ENLARGING
THE STORY

With Thanks
for the privilege
of being your colleague

Jim Pankratz
December 2005

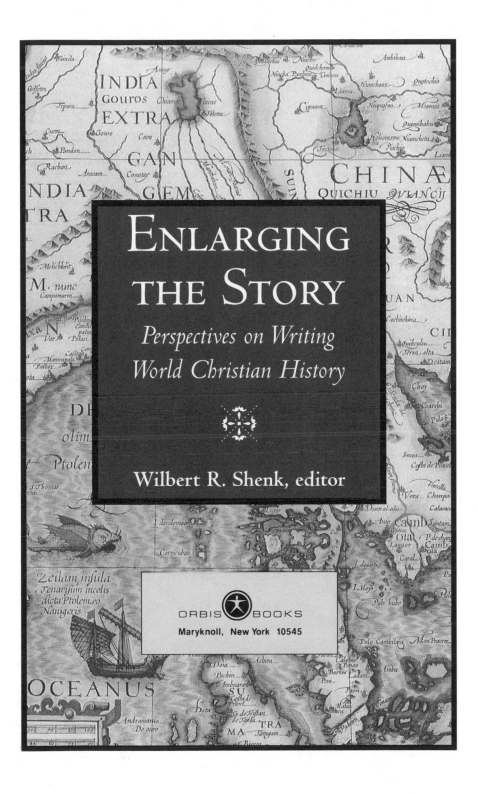

ENLARGING THE STORY

Perspectives on Writing World Christian History

Wilbert R. Shenk, editor

ORBIS BOOKS

Maryknoll, New York 10545

Founded in 1970, Orbis Books endeavors to publish works that enlighten the mind, nourish the spirit, and challenge the conscience. The publishing arm of the Maryknoll Fathers and Brothers, Orbis seeks to explore the global dimensions of the Christian faith and mission, to invite dialogue with diverse cultures and religious traditions, and to serve the cause of reconciliation and peace. The books published reflect the views of their authors and do not represent the official position of the Maryknoll Society.

To obtain more information about Maryknoll and Orbis Books, please visit our website at www.maryknoll.org.

Library of Congress Cataloging-in-Publication Data

Enlarging the story : perspectives on writing world Christian history / Wilbert R. Shenk, editor.
     p.   cm.
   Includes bibliographical references and index.
   ISBN 1-57075-453-5 (pbk.)
   1. Church history – Study and teaching. 2. Missions – History.
I. Shenk, Wilbert R.
BR138 .E55 2002
270'.07'2 – dc21

                                          2002005733

Contents

Acknowledgments

Grateful acknowledgment is made to the Henry W. Luce Foundation and Fieldstead and Company for generous grants that made possible the convening of an international symposium in which forty-five historians and missiologists from all continents participated on the theme "Towards a Global Christian History." Fuller Theological Seminary, Pasadena, California, served as host for this event held April 30–May 2, 1998. Without this support the symposium and subsequent preparation and publication of this book would not have been possible.

Contributors

PABLO DEIROS is Professor of the History of Missions, Fuller Theological Seminary, and continues to teach in several graduate schools in Argentina. Among his numerous publications is *Historia del Cristianismo en América Latina* (1992).

MARK HUTCHINSON is head of the History and Society Program and Dean of Graduate Studies, Southern Cross College, and an associate of the School of History, Macquarrie University. He has published widely on Australian religious and immigration history. His most recent book is *Iron in Our Blood: A History of the Presbyterian Church in New South Wales* (Sydney: Ferguson Press, 2001).

KLAUS KOSCHORKE is Professor of Church History in the Faculty of Evangelical Theology, University of Munich. He serves as an editor of the series "Studies in the History of Christianity in the Non-Western World" and edited the volume *"Christen und Gewuerze": Konfrontation und Interacktion Kolonialer und Indigener Christentumsvarianten* (Göttingen: Vandenhoeck and Ruprecht, 1998).

PHILIP YUEN-SANG LEUNG is Professor of History and Director of the Research Institute for the Humanities, Chinese University of Hong Kong. The author of seven books, he is currently writing a book to be titled *Rethinking Culture in Contemporary China*, a study of Confucianism, Christianity, and Communism in China today.

DONALD M. LEWIS, Professor of Church History, Regent College, Vancouver, British Columbia, has published several works in the field of the history of evangelicalism and was editor of *The Blackwell Dictionary of Evangelical Biography*, 2 vols. (Oxford, U.K., and Cambridge, Mass.: Blackwell, 1995).

MELBA MAGGAY is Director of the Institute for Studies in Asian Church and Culture, Quezon City, Philippines, and active in research projects in the Philippines as well as internationally.

A. MATHIAS MUNDADAN, C.M.I., Professor Emeritus, Dharmaram Vidya Kshetram (Bangalore), is Director, Acharya Palackal Jeevass Kendram, St. Antony's Monastery, Aluva, Kerala, India. His recent publications include *History and Beyond* (1997) and *Paths of Indian Theology* (1998).

GERALD J. PILLAY is Foundation Professor of Theology and Dean of the School of Liberal Arts at the University of Otago, Dunedin, New Zealand. Among his publications are *Perspectives on Church History* (1991) and *Religion at the Limits* (1994). He is presently working on *Christianity in the Modern World.*

LAMIN SANNEH, D. Willis James Professor of Missions and World Christianity, Yale University, New Haven, Connecticut, has written widely on the history of religion, Islam, and Christianity in Africa. He is author of *Abolitionists Abroad: American Blacks and the Making of Modern West Africa* (2000).

WILBERT R. SHENK is the Paul E. Pierson Professor of Mission History and Contemporary Christianity, Fuller Theological Seminary, Pasadena, California, and has written *Changing Frontiers of Mission* (1999).

ANDREW F. WALLS is Professor Emeritus in the Centre for the Study of Christianity in the Non-Western World, University of Edinburgh, and author of *The Missionary Movement in Christian History* (1996) and *The Cross-Cultural Process in Christian History* (2001).

Introduction

Wilbert R. Shenk

The way we understand and define the present determines how we interpret the past. If the present is nothing more than the seamless unfolding, a continual working out, of the worldview and forces that have been at play in our culture over the past several centuries, we will emphasize continuity. But if we observe that history's river has overflowed its traditional banks and is cutting new channels, then the emphasis falls on discontinuity and we recognize that our interpretive framework must be modified if we are to do justice to this dynamic reality.

This volume is based on the premise that Christian reality has reached a new high-water mark and is overflowing the banks of its traditional riverbed. Changes over the past two hundred years have been so massive that we have no choice but to rethink how the history and development of the church is to be conceptualized and interpreted. If we are to have a viable understanding of the church as we head into the twenty-first century, we have no choice but to reassess the nature and scope of Christianity as a global faith. At the beginning of the third millennium, three dimensions stand out that only a hundred years ago could not have been imagined: (a) the shift from being a Eurocentric church to a polycentric one; (b) the multiple sources of growth — biological, missionary, indigenous dynamics; (c) the dynamic social, political, and economic environment that has contributed to this rapid change.

(a) **From Eurocentric to polycentric.** The empirical basis for the work presented here (Figures 1 and 2) can be established by noting key developments of the past two hundred years. As Figure 1 shows graphically, world population has undergone a veritable explosion, growing from 902 million in 1800 to six billion in 2000. The year 1800 is also roughly the beginning of the modern mission movement. Two additional facts can be correlated with this demographic change. First, in 1800, Christians were approximately 23 percent of the total population (Figures 1 and 2). A century later, the percentage of

Figure I. World Population and Christian Growth since 1800

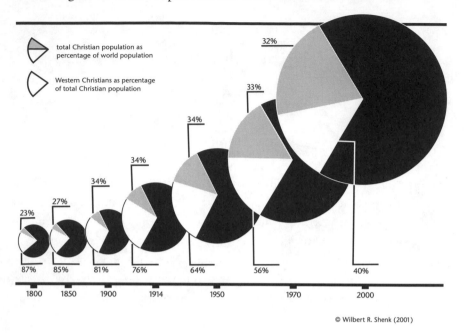

© Wilbert R. Shenk (2001)

Christians had risen to some 34 percent. Second, the profile of the world Christian community changed significantly between 1800 and 2000. This is the kind of shift that occurs but rarely. In 1800, 87 percent of all Christians were located in Europe and North America, and Europe was regarded as the Christian "heartland." By 1914, a barely visible new trend had started. The percentage of all Christians who were European–North American had declined to 76 percent. This trend continued so that by 1970 just 56 percent of all Christians were in Europe and North America. Around 1980, Christian adherents were evenly divided between Europe–North America, on the one hand, Asia, Africa, Latin America, and Oceania, on the other, with the growth momentum on the side of the non-Western church.

At the beginning of the third millennium the impact of this historical shift is clear: 60 percent of all Christians live outside the traditional Western heartland. Both the scope and speed of this change can only be described as astonishing. Clearly, the onrushing Christian reality in the third millennium is finding multiple new channels. The traditional interpretive framework is completely inadequate to describe and interpret the pluriform Christian reality that makes up the church today.

Figure 2. Global Status of World Population and Christianity[1]

Year	Total Population (millions)	Christian Population (millions)	Christians as Percentage of Total Population	Non-Western/ Western Christians (percent)	Languages in Which Scriptures Are Available
33	170	0			
500			22	62/38	13
950	193	43	19	41/59	17
1000	269	50			
1350	360	87	24	32/68	28
1500	425	81	19	7/93	23
1750	721	160	22	15/85	60
1800	903	208			
1815			24	14/86	86
1900	1,620	558			
1914			34	24/76	676
1950	2,510	856	34	36/64	1,052
1970	3,696	1,236	34	44/56	
1980					1,811
1990	5,266	1,747	33	56/44	
2000	6,055	2,000	32	60/40	2,092[2]

1. David B. Barrett, ed., *World Christian Encyclopedia* (Nairobi: Oxford University Press, 1982 and 2000).

2. R. D. Shaw, "Bible Translation," in *Evangelical Dictionary of World Missions*, A. Scott Moreau et al., eds. (Grand Rapids, Mich.: Baker, 2000).

The task of historical interpretation must be brought into line with this new reality. The assumptions that have governed our understanding of Christian history during the past several centuries were all formed in the European context where the church was identified with the cultural and religious majority and attention was focused largely on its institutional life. Western Christians long ago came to regard this as the norm. As the churches in Europe and North America sent missionaries to other parts of the world, it was believed that these Western forms and norms unquestionably applied to all churches founded by the missionaries throughout the world.

Today these long-held assumptions are being contested and Western Christian reality is in a liminal state. Historical forces are laying siege to the central conceptions that have for so long and so powerfully supported the European Christian tradition at home and in its multiple extensions worldwide. The West, the Christian "heartland" for the past millennium, is being superseded. The non-Western Christian preponderance is the product of a combination of two facts: the decline in Christian affiliation in the West and continued growth in Asia, Africa, and Latin America. This ecclesiastical change has coincided with equally decisive geopolitical changes following the collapse of the Soviet bloc and the continued erosion of Western political dominance.

(b) **Sources of growth.** A pressing need is for new theories concerning church growth and decline. In so-called Christian societies, Christian membership is essentially the same as the population and church growth is a correlate of biological growth. One consequence of the modern mission movement has been to focus attention on the growth of an indigenous church in a population where there had been no church. More recently, as the fact of substantial attrition in the Western Christian heartland has come to be acknowledged, causes of church decline have also been queried.

Church growth can be linked to three sources. The first, biological growth, has already been noted. The other two are missionary initiative and indigenous agency. One of the criticisms leveled at mission studies is that these studies have failed to acknowledge the extent to which all missionary work has been a team effort. The missionary has been dependent on the collaboration of indigenous evangelists, catechists, Bible women, and lay workers. Yet mission studies have typically featured the missions and missionaries. This major imbalance must surely be acknowledged. The resulting interpretation has often been one-sided and seriously flawed. However, the missionary has been an actor in the drama of the modern mission movement. It simply will not do to react by writing the missionary out of the story. A balanced and honest approach is needed that accounts for all participants in the process.

The third source of church growth, especially in the past two centuries, has been indigenous agency. This includes a range of movements, with only indirect ties to Christian churches, led by indigenous evangelists, prophets, and healers that are attracting large numbers of people. Accounts of such movements were published early in the nineteenth century, but scholars have been reluctant to include these phenomena in Christian history.[1] One solution has been to bracket the problem by treating these indigenous Christian movements as a subset of mission history on the assumption that mission history was qualitatively different from church history.

The purpose of these remarks is to suggest that the processes of growth

---

1. See Geoffrey A. Oddie, "India: Missionaries, Conversion, and Change," *The Church Mission Society and World Christianity, 1799–1999* (Grand Rapids, Mich.: Eerdmans, 2000), 229–53. Oddie studies the interaction between missionaries and indigenous movements in early nineteenth-century India.

need to be reconsidered if we are to have a more adequate understanding of the development of the church in the modern period.

(c) **The sociopolitical environment.** Whether measured in terms of the growth of population since 1800 — from approximately 900 million to more than six billion two centuries later — or the scope of political change in this period, the sociopolitical environment has been marked by great dynamism. This is the period of the rise of the modern city, industrialization, the technological revolution, and transformed transportation and communications systems. The present system of nation-states is a late development. Historians are calling the twentieth century the most violent on record. These randomly selected observations point to the fact that the environment of the past two centuries has been dynamically unstable. Although religion has not disappeared from the modern world as social science theorists predicted earlier, the role of religion in this culture has changed. What does it mean that the Christian movement has apparently fared best over the past two hundred years among the poor, the young, and the non-Western peoples of the world?

A critical issue facing the Christian movement worldwide is that of *identity*. Western Christians long assumed their religious identity was essentially the same as their cultural identity. Now they are awakening to the fact that this is no longer a possibility. Christians from other continents face a different set of circumstances. From the beginning they have carried the burden of living under censure, stigmatized as being disloyal to family and nation. Thus, Christians from different parts of the world and with contrasting histories now face the common challenge of forging a viable Christian identity for the next millennium. The vast majority of Christians throughout the world now find themselves living as minorities in societies that are pluralist or where other religions and ideologies dominate. An indispensable resource for working out this identity is the historical experience of the church of the past several centuries.

This volume originated in an international symposium hosted by Fuller Theological Seminary and held in Pasadena, California, April 30–May 2, 1998, attended by forty-five historians and missiologists from all continents. Only a part of the rich materials presented, discussed, and debated at the symposium is presented here.

In broad strokes Andrew F. Walls describes the historical trajectory that brought Christians to where they are at present using materials borrowed from Greek philosophy, Roman law, and the tribal cultures of the Germanic and Slavic peoples. Out of this amalgam were forged the forms and thought world that constituted Christendom. This remained the dominant form of Christianity until the modern period. The transition to modernity triggered a fundamental transformation. The missionary movement took the Christian message to all corners of the non-Western world for the purpose of founding the church where it had never been. At the same time it was becoming apparent that the church in the West was losing vitality, and in the twentieth century the Western church sustained a steady loss in adherents. In spite of this decisive change in Christian reality, the syllabus for church history continues to be oriented to the Western tradition. Walls uses the example of the church history syllabus to make the larger point that Western theological and historical hegemony continues to block the way to a full-orbed understanding of Christian reality today. It is as if the West, recognizing that theological education is the last stronghold of Western control, instinctively refuses to surrender this vestige of a bygone dominance. Yet in view of this drastically changed Christian reality, we cannot evade the task of reconceptualizing the historical task. Failure to do so will leave us with a distorted — even false — view of the Christian movement during the past two centuries — one of the most dynamic periods in all Christian history.

Fortunately, there is ferment among church historians. An increasing number are recognizing the impact of globalization on geopolitical relations. The Christian movement must be set within this vast network of multilateral connections that operate at local, regional, national, and global levels. As Fr. A. M. Mundadan makes clear, this changing environment is creating a new historical consciousness that is best worked out by approaching church history as "encounter and assimilation." That is to say, what is required is to study the way the Christian message interacts with all the cultures it encounters. Drawing on the work that has been done in India since the 1970s, Mundadan shows how the practice of church history within its multiple contexts can serve the church's need to clarify its nature and mission.

The Western church historiographical tradition was based on a dichotomy with church history on the one side and mission history on the other. Mission history was concerned with Christian activity outside the West. Church history treated the life and work of the church in the West. Using his own experience as a starting point, Philip Leung tellingly deconstructs this dichotomous view that is even more untenable today than it was in the past. The historian who is searching for truth and reality is engaged in a quest for self-understanding. The Christian historian in a country like China, where the Christian faith, as a small minority, has always had a tenuous relationship with the dominant culture, has to recognize the various cultural mentalities that are present and that rightfully sue for recognition in any historical account, whether that be cultural, religious, or political.

While the conceptual sorting-out process must continue, we are compelled to address other issues, including how a *re*-formed historiography is to be taught and the curriculum that will be its basis. Gerald Pillay recognizes that in the classroom today we must work with students whose sensibilities have been formed by the forces of globalization, postmodernity, and pluralism. Old assumptions and constructs will not work. For example, the time-honored distinction that has been drawn between religious and secular history creates confusion today. If we are concerned to demonstrate how the church must be present in society in order to bear faithful witness, we must find ways of interpreting this relationship, rather than denying it. Christian history ought to be taught so as to expose students to the multiple dimensions of what is a dynamic process, one that reaches to all points on the compass. Both a new curriculum and a new pedagogy are needed.

In his meditation on the nexus between *world* Christianity and the *new* historiography, Lamin Sanneh emphasizes that it is incumbent on the historian to lead the way in subverting the West's "claims to primacy" as to how the history of the Christian movement should be presented since this Western version falsifies the account. We have long depended on such history because the unrecorded voices of Bible women, evangelists, catechists, translators, and uncounted faithful laypeople had apparently been lost to history. This gap — this historical amnesia — can no longer be justified. A major part of the task in the future will be to revise the accounts by filling in what has been omitted heretofore. The goal of a global historiography must be to allow all voices to be heard. In this sense, revision is supremely the act of retrieval of that which has been missing, and that in two senses. First, the accounts we have depended on have been unbalanced and incomplete. In the second place, these partial accounts have hidden from view the fullness of the gospel as it has encountered diverse peoples for whom it was fresh and welcomed as good news. The "point of contact" has varied from one group to another. Each has responded because the gospel spoke to them in their particular situation and sense of need. For the Western multitudes now immunized against the gospel and who therefore reject it, the strongest word of challenge comes from those peoples from other continents who within the past generation or two have found that gospel to be a life-sustaining resource in the midst of poverty, oppression, and disintegrating traditional cultures.

ONE

EUSEBIUS TRIES AGAIN

The Task of Reconceiving and Re-visioning
the Study of Christian History

Andrew F. Walls

The most striking feature of Christianity at the beginning of the third millennium is that it is predominantly a non-Western religion. For all present indications, the numbers of inhabitants of Europe and North America who profess the faith are declining, as they have been for some time, while the churches of the other continents continue to grow. Already more than half the world's Christians live in Africa, Asia, Latin and Caribbean America, and the Pacific. If present trends continue, at some point in the twenty-first century, the figure could be two-thirds. It seems that the representative Christianity of the twenty-first century will be that of Africa, Asia, Latin and Caribbean America, and the Pacific; it is at least possible that the Christianity of Europe may become increasingly a matter of historical reference. The events which, for its weal or for its woe, will shape the Christianity of the early centuries of the next millennium are those already taking place in Africa, Asia, and Latin America. We have long been used to a Christian theology that was shaped by the interaction of Christian faith with Greek philosophy and Roman law. We are equally accustomed, though not usually so conscious of its origins, to ecclesiology and codes of practice shaped by Christian interaction with the traditional law and custom of the Germanic and Slavic tribes beyond the Roman frontiers. These forms have become so familiar and established that we have come to think of them as the normal and characteristic forms of Christianity. In the coming century we can expect an accelerated process of new development arising from Christian interaction with the ancient cultures of Africa and Asia, an interaction now in progress but with much further to go.

That Christianity from being a Western religion has become a non-Western one is striking only for the suddenness and rapidity of the transition.

Latourette spoke of the nineteenth century as the great century of missions, but it is the twentieth that has been the most remarkable for the transformation of Christianity. One has to go back many centuries to find a parallel to such a huge recession in one part of the world, such a huge simultaneous accession in another, producing the radical shift in the cultural and demographic composition of the Christian church that has occurred since 1900. Yet it took Christianity a long time to become a Western religion, let alone *the* Western religion. It did not begin as a Western religion (in the usual significance of that word), and it took many centuries to become thoroughly appropriated in Europe. It was still later that Christianity became so singularly associated with Europe — and Europe alone — as to be thought of as a European religion. Indeed it was not until comparatively recent times — around the year 1500 — that the ragged conversion of the last pagan peoples of Europe, the overthrow of Muslim power in Spain, and the final eclipse of Christianity in Central Asia and Nubia combined to produce a Europe that was essentially Christian and a Christianity that was essentially European. Paradoxically it is just at this point, when Europe and Christianity were more closely identified with each other than ever before, that the impact of the non-Western world upon the Western became critical. In the very era in which Western Christianity became fully and confidently formulated, the process which was to lead to its transformation or supersession had begun.

I speak deliberately of the impact of the non-Western world upon the West, rather than the other way around because, for the topic of the rewriting of church history, that is the more important aspect of the story. New church history writing must deal with the interaction between a Christianity formulated in relation to Western needs and conditions and a whole series of other cultures with histories of their own. If church history writing is to recount the whole story of the faith of Christ, it must explore how that story has, since the sixteenth century, been determined, directly or indirectly, by the worlds which first burst upon Western Christian consciousness at that time. Not until the twentieth century did it become clear how substantial that impact had been. And the task of catching up with that development academically has hardly yet begun.

It is not only a task for the theological disciplines. When I began academic work relating to Africa some forty years ago, religion was a marginal area of African studies. The primal religions of Africa were still largely considered to be the domain of the anthropologist. A place could be allowed for Islamic studies as a specialized area. But as regards Christianity in Africa, only what were then beginning to be called African Independent churches could be regarded as properly African. The rest of African Christianity could be subsumed under the heading "missions" (*The Missionary Factor in East Africa* is the title of one of the distinguished studies published in the 1950s). Any study of "missions" was likely to be about external influences on Africa. This period of academic study saw the beginning of decolonization and the emergence of the new African states. It was, and is, recognized that the missions influenced these events through the education of the elite who led the movement to independence, and through the organizational and leadership structures of the churches. In general, however, the undoubted Christian influences on the pan-African revolution of the 1950s and 1960s — when study of Christianity was largely the study of "missions" — were indirect, often unconscious, sometimes unintentional. A generation later, in the late 1980s and early 1990s, a second pan-African revolution took place, as dictators and military regimes in different parts of the continent were overthrown and a new South Africa emerged out of Africa's seemingly most intractable situation. In this second revolution, in country after country, the churches were vehicles of change, or catalysts in times of transition, or acted as umpires on behalf of society. Time after time, the churches of Africa preserved a viable form of civil society when other forms had collapsed or been suppressed. The phenomena can be observed in countries as different as Benin and Zambia; even in an overwhelmingly Muslim setting such as Mali, a Christian bishop acted as keeper of the national conscience. Political scientists in the African field found a knowledge of church structures to be a necessary part of their equipment. Christianity has now become so much a part of the fabric of sub-Saharan African life that anyone who wants to undertake serious study of Africa needs to know something about Christianity. The converse is equally true; anyone who wishes to undertake serious study of Christianity these days needs to know something about Africa.

It follows that the student of Christian history must not only know something about Africa, but consider the part that Africa plays in the total story of the faith. And the issue is much wider than that of Africa; it goes to the heart of the task of the global church historian. What follows is not meant as a complete list, even of priorities, but it offers plenty to occupy us. The names assigned may appear contrived and are certainly open to improvement, but they all stand for dimensions of the church historian's work as the third Christian millennium dawns. Two will be dealt with here: they are reconception and re-visioning. Two others follow from them: research and re-commissioning.

Reconception

What conceptions govern the present study and teaching of Christian history, and to what extent does the contemporary situation of Christianity call for adjustment or replacement?

It is difficult here to avoid intruding an autobiographical note. The justification I offer is the old-fashioned Methodist requirement to provide an account of one's conversion and call to preach. Three episodes come particularly to mind. The first occurred in West Africa while I was in my early thirties. I had been appointed to teach church history. My training for the purpose could be counted impeccable; what better exposure could the younger churches (as they were called in those days) have than to the ripe experience of the older churches, and especially of their oldest period? I had done my graduate work in patristics at Oxford, a temple of patristic study, and under the great F. L. Cross, its high priest. What I lacked, however, was something all my students already possessed, the actual experience of living in a second-century church.

My early life as a teacher, seeking to impart the "lessons" of early church history, was somewhat frustrating; my rich compensation came from developing an acquaintance with the local church and society. The students, of course, wrote down all I said; it was part of the ritual transfer of knowledge. Yet all the while they possessed keys which might have opened new doors into vexing questions about apostolic tradition, whereas I had only secondhand accounts of earlier versions of those questions. I doubt if I did much good in my first five years as a church history teacher in Africa, but I am everlastingly grateful that I learned there that second-century Christianity (and third-century and first-century Christianity) can still be witnessed and shared in. A saying of F. L. Cross, my revered teacher, brought further illumination. "We know next to nothing about the ante-Nicene church." He was right, as he usually was. But we now have better resources for understanding the patchwork of fragments of Christian literature that survive from before the age of the great councils by examining the recent histories of the churches of Africa and Asia than the Bodleian or the Vatican libraries can yield. The same themes, often the same media, occur:

- earnest and rather turgid moral homilies (much of Romans 12–16, little of Romans 1–8);

- eloquent episcopal letters equally displaying autocratic temper and moving self-sacrifice;

- apocalyptic visions of the fate of church members who behave badly;

- guidance on discerning the spirits (a prophet whose "word from the Lord" is to order a meal for himself is a false prophet, a prophet who outstays reasonable hospitality is a false prophet);

- cheerful fictional correspondence between Jesus and a local king showing how early this particular locality accepted the gospel;

- decisions of synods determining who had what relations with which government officials, now discredited;

- regulations about exorcising the water prior to baptism;

- and gospels with bigger and better miracles than the canonical ones.

These came with heart-moving testimony and muckraking scandal, coded utterances, gnomic memorials, and thought-provoking graffiti. All readily find analogies, and sometimes replications, in the recent and contemporary history of the churches that are now in their first and second centuries of existence.

I yield to no one in desiring that the theological libraries of Africa and Asia, of Latin America and the Pacific be equipped to bear the responsibilities in Christian scholarship that are theirs. But the scholars of those areas will have resources in their own experience, and in the present and recent experience of their churches, that may provide deeper insight than we have yet had into the surviving literature of ante-Nicene Christianity. The whole delirious mixture: the proliferation of local varieties, the official and popular faces of the church, its moderates and its radicals, its bridge builders and its pacesetters, its interaction with the mind-sets of the synagogue and the academy, and the club and the street corner. Latter-day Protestants, nourished on the legacy of the sixteenth-century Reformation, are sometimes struck by the transition from the Apostle of the Gentiles to the Apostolic Fathers. How is it that leaders of churches associated with Paul, who treasured his words and revered his memory, people to whom we owe the very preservation of the Pauline letters — and who knew Greek better than we do — seemed to have no idea of what we think Paul means by "justification by faith"? Scholars coming from the new second-century churches will probably see no puzzle at all.

The first aspect of the first task, reconception, is thus to reconceive the resources available for its study. There are rich possibilities in rereading earlier history in the light of the living experience of the churches of the southern continents.

The second aspect is suggested by a second phase of my "conversion and call to preach." After almost a decade in Africa, I was again teaching church history, but in the theological faculty of an ancient Scottish university, in a course designed principally for candidates for the ministry of the Church of Scotland. The course was solidly planned and executed, demanding three years' study of church history. The first year was devoted to study of the early church (a concept which we must examine in a moment). The second year was concerned with the Reformation — the Church of Scotland is a Reformed church. (Notice how effortless is the transition from Augustine to Luther, how cursory the consideration of the period in which Scotland, and most of Northern Europe, became Christian. Few Western theologians get much background about the origins of Western Christianity from their church history course.) The third year was, of course, devoted to Scotland. There could hardly be a clearer statement of the purpose of a degree course in church history: it is the understanding of *us* as *we* are.

The general scope of this course, reflecting and incorporating the work of formidable scholars, had probably changed little over the twentieth century. What had changed over that time, of course, was the shape of the Christian constituency. A person following that course could gain an excellent grasp of how the Church of Scotland came to be what it was. But what hope would they have of understanding the true nature of the twentieth-century church of which Scottish Christians were a part? What mental space was there to take in the idea of a world church in which Scotland was on the outside edge? Everything in ministerial training conspired to promote the idea that Scotland was at the center. But the students following the course, preparing for the ministry, were aware that the Church of Scotland was a church in recession, losing members every year since 1950. The teaching of church history implicitly emphasized decline: a glorious past, an uncertain future. What hope would Scottish congregations so served ever have of learning the truth about the church?

The traditional Scottish church history syllabus of that day, if a rather blatant example of the genre, exhibited in conception and design the general features of most Western church history syllabuses. These provide a selection of topics designed to exhibit a particular tradition. Usually that tradition is partly geographical — that is, the selection represents influences bearing on a particular locality — Scotland, Germany, or North America. The geographical bias starts early; early church syllabuses tend to lose interest in the Greek-speaking church — though it was still the largest sector of Christianity —

after the great creedal controversies. The reason is, of course, that Scottish, German, and American Christianity were more directly affected by events in the Latin-speaking area. And in this, as in other cases, the geographical bias reinforces a linguistic and cultural one. The other main principle of selection is confessional: the church which is the subject of church history is implicitly defined as the church we ourselves know — *our* "tradition" as it has developed.

In principle, there is no harm in this, provided we know what we are doing, and provided also we do more than this. It is natural and right to seek to understand one's own tradition; it is the means to know who one's ancestors are. But there are lurking dangers, both historical and theological. One is that we think by study of our own tradition we are doing church history. We are not — we are doing *our* church history. If this is the only lens through which we study Christian history, we have bypassed the story of the whole people of God in favor of clan history. This reduces the area in which we look for the works of God, whereas the promises of God are to all who trust in them. The Lord of Hosts is not to be treated as a territorial Baal.

The second reason arises from inertia. There is little internal compulsion to review the construction of one's historical framework as conditions change. This was the case with the Scottish example mentioned earlier; a framework that fairly interpreted the tradition around 1910 no longer did so sixty years later. As a result, the students, and the congregations beyond them, were actually being prevented from understanding their *own* church history. They were part of a larger, more dynamic Christian movement than they could ever realize from their education.

There is a third danger. Not only may we think we are engaged in church history when it is only clan history; our version may be copied by people who have different ancestors. May I be allowed a third autobiographical incident — or rather series of incidents, for a similar experience has befallen me several times. The most vivid impression is of a workshop on the teaching of church history, consisting of seminary teachers from various parts of India, a few years ago. It soon became clear that those present were using versions of syllabuses originating in European or, more often, North American institutions. Most were also trying to teach some Indian or in some cases Asian church history; in most cases this was taught as a separate course. That is, there was church history and there was Asian church history (it was an entirely Protestant gathering); the latter, after the obligatory reference to St. Thomas, began in 1792. Church history was a given — the course a seamless robe into which Asia could not be sewn.

The striking thing about the gathering was that everyone seemed to realize that what they were doing was dire, that both they and the students were bored with the process of transmitting and receiving an assemblage of facts that were completely unrelated to anything that actually excited any Indian Christian of today. But both teachers and students must persevere; their task was theological education, and church history was a constituent of theological education. And how could theological education continue without one of its principal constituent disciplines?

If the traditional Western church history syllabus is defective and obscuring for Western Christians, how much more stultifying is it for African and Asian Christians? The problem is not so much that it does not contain African or Asian church history, as that it provides no framework in which either can be considered.

If the first aspect of reconception is the reconception of resources, the second must surely be the reconception of syllabus. There is no way in which African and Asian church history can be incorporated within a traditional Western-type syllabus; nor can they be treated as appendages to Western church history. But there is a more fundamental issue which affects church history teaching in any setting. If Christianity is principally a non-Western religion, why should its Western period dominate the approach to its history?

How great that dominance has been can be divined if we examine more closely the assumptions underlying the standard forms of syllabus which have been exported all over the world. For instance, the majority of institutions provide courses on the history of the early church. It is safe to assume that in most cases the "early church" means, substantially, the church in the Roman Empire. Undoubtedly, Western Christianity, Catholic and Protestant (and for that matter Greek and Russian Orthodox, too), were shaped by events that took place in the church's interaction with Hellenistic civilization and the Roman state. As Eusebius, the first great church historian, recognized, the conversion of Constantine marks a turning point, a turning of the tide, a new epoch.

But suppose we look at early Christianity outside the Roman Empire? Suppose we look not only at the well-known movement westward from Antioch but the eastward movement as well? The little buffer state of Osrhoene, on the Roman imperial frontier, was the early base of a remarkable Christian movement. In Edessa, its capital, are the remains of the oldest church building yet discovered, built at a time when no such thing was possible in the Roman Empire. Edessa, indeed, often does appear on maps of the early church. Unfortunately, it is usually at the eastern extremity of the map, yielding the idea that it represents the eastern extremity of a Christianity centered on the Mediterranean. If, however, we place Edessa at the western end of the map, and pigeonhole the Roman Empire for a while, we can observe a remarkable alternative Christian story.

Early Christianity spread down the Euphrates Valley until the majority of the population of Northern Mesopotamia (modern Iraq) was Christian. It spread through the Arab buffer states, so that a third-century poet can announce that the social customs of the desert Arabs have changed, and exposure of children has ceased. It moved down to Yemen and was adopted by the royal house. It moved steadily into Iran proper, into the Zoroastrian heartland of Fars, and northward to the Caspian. (It had previously moved west of the Caspian; the first nation to adopt Christianity as its state religion was not the Roman Empire but the Kingdom of Armenia.)

This Eastern Christianity that grew up in the Persian Empire had much in common with the form of the faith that was developing in the same period in the Greco-Roman world. But its cultural milieu was quite different. Like the earliest church of all, it was Semitic in language and in cast of thought, retaining some of the features of that earliest church that were lost in the development of Hellenistic Christianity. Its immediate milieu was not solely Hellenistic, and its earliest leaders show little interest in the issues that so exercised those who were trying to translate the gospel and the convictions associated with it into Greek terms. Arius caused hardly a ripple. With much less need to work with the categories and methods of philosophical discourse, these Christians had to take account of a range of indigenous and Eastern religious influences, including the effect of the Zoroastrian influence in local culture. There emerged a religion of intense moral seriousness, of spiritual athleticism, that spoke to a community marked by the eternal conflict of the principles of Light and Darkness, and the realities of death and judgment. There developed a literature which gloried in displaying Christ's victory over death and evil, rich poetic theology, and striking imagery, such as we find in Ephrem's magnificent taunting songs about the defeat of humanity's two discredited enemies, Death and Satan.

Like their fellow Christians in the Roman Empire, Eastern Christians fell foul of the principalities and powers. The persecutions under Decius and Diocletian are a well-known feature of the story of Christianity of the Roman Empire; the Christians of the Persian Empire knew still fiercer and more sustained pressure. In one forty-year period of the fourth century, no less than sixteen thousand Christians were put to death by the Persian Emperor Sapor II.

The cause for this particularly savage attack on Christians was a direct response to Constantine's Edict of Toleration and the increasing favor shown to Christians thereafter. Anything so appealing to the Roman state as Christianity had now become could hardly appeal to Rome's perennial enemy. The critical difference between the story of Christianity in the Persian Empire and that in the Roman Empire is that the Persian Empire never had a Constantine. Eastern Christianity never knew steady imperial favor or predictable political security. That in itself makes it a story worth studying along with that of its Roman neighbor.

Eastern Christianity had, however, its periods of peace and substantial seasons of growth. It spread not only through but beyond the Persian Empire, along the trade routes by sea and by land. Its age-old presence in India is well known, its presence beyond India — in Sri Lanka, for instance — documented. That Eastern Christianity reached China is also often recognized; those interested in synchronous parallels might note that the missionary whose Chinese name was A Lo Pen arrived in the capital of the T'ang Emperor in 635, much the same time as the faith was put before the king and council of Northumbria in northern England. Indeed, if we are thinking in terms of geographical extent, the eastward spread of the Christian faith across Asia is still more remarkable than the westward spread across Europe.

That spread was sustained through a period which in Western church history is substantially one of loss and decline. The arrival of the Muslim Arabs in Egypt and Syria, the Eastern provinces of the Roman Empire, marks the beginning of a period of eclipse — Latourette's "thousand years of uncertainty." Further east, Christianity was allowed a new period of flowering, so that the tenth century begins a time of Christian growth. Right up to the fourteenth century the expansion of the faith went on among the shamanistic Turkic peoples who surrounded the Chinese Empire. It is a period little understood and the sources difficult to access; yet if we could understand it better, we might gain some clues to developments of much later periods — perhaps, for instance, some features of Korean Christianity which also has a shamanistic background. One striking feature of the period is that during it, Christianity became the faith of nomadic peoples. Many of the Turkic peoples were pastoralists on the move. We hear of bishops appointed to such peoples who had no fixed capital; they moved with their communities. In the modern period of missionary endeavor, it is hard to find examples of nomadic communities who embraced the gospel and remained nomadic.

If we look at the eastward as well as the westward Christian movement, and look at it on the grids of the Persian and Chinese Empires as well as on that of the Roman Empire, it is evident that there was almost a millennium and a half of Christian history in Asia before Western Christian missions to Asia began. And that Christian history is not a marginal or ephemeral one, but substantial. The ancestors of modern Asian Christianity exist, but their names are not being called. And both Western and Asian Christians will remain impoverished by this until the work of reconception of the syllabus progresses.

African church history is equally distorted by attempts to make it an appendage of a "general" church history which is really a form of European clan history. Africa has a continuous Christian history since sub-apostolic times, a history that antedates not only Western missions to Africa but the Islamic presence there. It is important for African Christian consciousness that this is reflected in the syllabus. Even that part of African Christianity that lay within the Roman Empire has its ongoing importance, not least because, in Egypt, it has continued to the present day. The sheer luxuriance of early African Christianity is worth noticing. It was the source of such seminal figures as Origen, the first systematic theologian, and Tertullian, the first theologian of Pentecostalism. It was the birthplace alike of vernacular theology and of Western theology through those African lawyer-theologians Tertullian, Cyprian, and Augustine, and the source of innovative socially conscious Christian movements like Donatism, which perhaps produced the first liberation theologians. We dare not separate these from modern Christianity in Africa, any more that we can separate sub-Saharan Africa from the lands to its north. There are geopolitical forces which tie the whole continent together. In our own day, Islam has become the focus of those forces. It is worth recalling that Christianity, too, once had a similar role in African history.

The Christianity of Egypt and Roman Africa normally reaches the standard syllabus. Equally significant for Africa is an aspect of early African church history that rarely does: the Christian movement there outside the Roman Empire. With all the uncertainties and deficiencies of the sources, we have enough material (with archaeology providing much that was not available to our predecessors) to illuminate one chapter of African Christian history that lasted nearly a millennium, and another that has continued to the present. The thousand-year chapter is that of Nubia. This Christian community in what is now Sudan antedated the rise of Islam by five hundred years, and then held a unique place as a Christian state on the borders of the Islamic world.

The continuing story is, of course, that of Ethiopia. That story begins with the Syrian brothers, Frumentius and Aedesius, deflected from their original purpose when stranded in Axum in what is now Tigre, entering the service of the king and eventually seeing not only a church emerging but the conversion of the king. Again the archaeological sources illuminate the story; King Ezana's inscriptions show his progress from polytheist to monotheist to Christian. The continuation of the story has many other surprises and many mysteries. A tradition of Christianity grew up in the heart of Africa, in daily contact with the realities of African worldviews, that was recognizably part of the Great Church, and yet quite unlike anything that developed elsewhere. Ethiopian Christianity has incorporated the Old Testament to a degree unusual among Christians, and its people have often lived under conditions reminiscent of those of the Old Testament. And yet Ethiopia, for all its distinctiveness and all its long years of isolation, never entirely lost contact with the church outside. The foundation story makes the point clear: Frumentius went to the nearest center of the Great Church to ask for a bishop for the church he had founded. The patriarch sent him back as bishop. That patriarch was Athanasius. Century after century afterward, the Ethiopian church drew its bishop — its only bishop — from Alexandria, thereby recognizing the universality of the church even in its very particular circumstances. The significance of Ethiopia for all African Christians, as symbol of Africa indigenously, primordially Christian, and as symbol of a Christian tradition completely independent of the West, has been seized all over the continent, as the countless churches and societies all over the continent that take "Ethiopian" as part of their title bear witness.

If the new situation calls for reconception of the object and content of the syllabus, it calls also for reconception of the significance of some elements within it. A single example must suffice. For Western Christians, the sixteenth-century Reformation — perhaps it would be better to say Reformations — is of defining significance, a watershed. In the total history of Christianity its significance may be different and not necessarily so defining. Certainly it continues to determine the outside affiliations and the church-consciousness of Christians across the world; but for some historical purposes the differences between the different types of Western Christians have been less significant than the similarities. This may be particularly true in tracing the place of Western Christianity in the non-Western world. From the point of view of Africa and Asia, the missionary movement, Catholic and Protestant, has been a single story since the sixteenth century, the Catholic Reformation and the Evangelical Revival alike necessary to it. Protestants as much as Catholics owe the conception of a missionary movement based on people sent to persuade and commend but unable to coerce to the first encounter of Western Christians with the non-Western world. The missionary movement emerged from the realization that Asia and Africa could not be won for Christ by the methods used to extend Christendom in Mexico and Peru.

In the West, it is possible to recount Catholic and Protestant histories separately from one another. In many parts of the world it is not; the stories interlock. The first Protestant missionary in China owed his first grounding in Chinese to the presence in the British Museum and the Royal Society of a translation of the Gospels and a Chinese-Latin dictionary made by Jesuit missionaries of an earlier century. He owed his first breakthrough in China to the assistance of Chinese Catholics. There is a single Christian story in China from the sixteenth century; nay, even that story needs its prologue in the movement which began nine centuries earlier when A Lo Pen and his Syriac-speaking colleagues reached the Emperor's court by way of Central Asia.

But there is another reason that we may need to reconceive the historical significance of the Reformation. We have become used to the assumption that Christianity exists in three more or less permanent modes: Roman Catholic, Protestant, and Orthodox. But these categories reflect events in Western history; they have in the West a significance that they cannot have in the non-Western world. They will continue to be valid outside the West as indicators of organization and affiliation, but it is likely that they will become less and less useful as descriptors. A large segment of African Christianity, for instance, cannot be called either Catholic or Protestant in any meaningful sense: it is simply African. What is more, its features are to be found among thousands of African believers whose affiliation is Catholic or Protestant. There are "traditions" in the Christian world community today which reflect modes of Christian existence in the same way as the labels Catholic, Protestant, and Orthodox have hitherto done. It seems likely that, if we are to acquire historical understanding of Christianity as a non-Western religion, the reconception of the categories by which Christians have been described will be required.

Re-visioning

A second task imposed by the attempt to write world Christian history might be described as "re-visioning." This clumsy neologism is intended to indicate processes whereby new visions of Christian history, its nature, its purpose, its characteristics, are obtained. The plural "visions" is here used advisedly — there are many, perhaps an infinity, of new visions of Christian history to be glimpsed if we use the whole range of perspectives which world Christian history, carried out from within a world community of Christians, will offer.

In what follows it is taken for granted that the church historian's task in the contemporary situation is to present a vision of Christian history which reflects its position as a faith represented all over the world. This in itself marks a departure from the current dominant model, which assumes that the crucial events and processes in Christian history were those which took place in the Mediterranean world in the early Christian centuries, and in the West thereafter, and that anything else is an optional extra, determined by local needs. This is not to say that some single standard means of presenting and teaching church history should be adopted all over the world; we have already seen that the inherent defect of the dominant model is the assumption that one single presentation has universal application. There will continue to be a need to take account of local relevance in the selection of themes and in judging what belongs to the foreground and what belongs to the background. But the consciousness that even one's own Christian history is part of a process which covers all six continents and occupies two millennia in itself is something we can legitimately call "re-visioning."

The visions must also allow for the processes of historical flow, not just assemblages of events. A vision of African Christian history as a continental process with a continuity from the days of the early church offers possibilities that are not open if observation is directed severally to the Christianity of the parts of the Roman world that included Africa, to the fruits of the Portuguese presence from the sixteenth century, and to the outcome of Western missions since the nineteenth. A vision of African Christian history that concentrates on African initiatives, responses, resistance, and appropriation is likely to offer more sense of flow, and coherence, more scope for typological consideration and development of paradigms for understanding, than one which essentially chronicles the progress of missions in Africa. The westward movement of Christianity in the early centuries is depicted often enough, but we get a fuller vision of flow if we look also at its contemporaneous eastward movement. A still fuller vision dawns if we see the contrast between the Roman and Persian Empires in the arena of state policy, or the contrast between the impact on Mediterranean Christianity of the Muslim invasion of the Eastern Roman Empire and the way in which the Muslim demolition of the Persian Empire favored Christian expansion in Central Asia. The vision might extend to the ambiguous relationship of the Mongol peoples with the Christian faith as both destroyer and protector, and their part in enabling Christendom's

Third Rome to emerge in Moscow, as its Second Rome at Constantinople fell into ruin.

For the same reason, the process of re-visioning will involve a readiness to explore intercontinental connections. Such an undertaking might allow a new appreciation of themes now seen only as incidental. A prime example is afforded by Afro-America, which links the Christian history of Europe, Africa, and both Americas. The Atlantic Slave Trade that brings the triangle so tragically into existence is an inescapable theme for Christian study. The story, with its ghastly aspects, is full of the most complex interrelationships between the continents, with the African diaspora at that center. We can trace the process by which in Brazil and so much of Latin America, Africa became incorporated into Catholic Christianity. We can trace the subsequent emergence of Africans who were able to make a mark on European Christendom, such as Lourenço de Silva de Mendonça who persuaded a pope to pronounce against the slave trade. Equally, we can trace the very different processes, with all their contradictions, by which Africans in North America and the Caribbean came to meet Protestant and especially Evangelical Christianity and produced a new and distinctive mode of Christian existence. Nor may we forget that there have been other religious effects of the meeting of Africa and America, in the shape of the powerful new post-Christian religions that developed in Brazil and Haiti and now flourish in North American cities. The early and middle nineteenth century produced Christians who were haunted by Atlantic slavery as an institution fashioned among Christians, an abomination of desolation standing where it ought not, people who saw huge missionary significance in the African Christian population of the Americas — almost the only significant African population they knew of. To a large extent they were justified: the missionary story of Afro-America is a remarkable one, and because of its long, complex, and dispersed nature, it has never been told in its entirety. It is a story that includes the impact of demobilized black soldiers in the evangelization of the populations of Jamaica, Trinidad, and the Bahamas. (It is not regularly remembered that it was to assist the work of such evangelists, and by the invitation of the black soldiers, that the Baptist mission was established in Jamaica.) It includes the Christian settlements established in Sierra Leone and Liberia, the former being of especially critical importance for the development and spread of Christianity in West Africa. It includes the Jamaican part in the origins of Ghana's cocoa industry. It includes the Brazilian emigration to Nigeria that forms a landmark in Catholic history there. It includes the whole, long, diffused Afro-American missionary presence in Africa, some of it channeled through African American, some through other agencies. (What was long known as the Scottish Calabar mission in Nigeria arose from an initiative in the Presbytery of Jamaica.) It includes a succession of notable preachers, teachers, and writers. It includes the effect of an African American education on a succession of Africans of the colonial period, of whom J. E. K. Aggrey was only one eminent example.

The nineteenth-century vision of the missionary significance of Afro-America was not fulfilled in quite the way its seers expected — visions rarely are. And perhaps in some shape it still awaits fulfillment. At any rate, Christian historians have yet to take full account of Afro-America, that large slice of Africa set down in the Americas.

Intercontinental connections are not always so explicit. Perhaps the religious history of Europe in the sixteenth century may cast light on that of Latin America in the twentieth; equally, contemporary Latin America may illuminate our understanding of both the Protestant and the Catholic Reformations of four centuries ago. Perhaps the topic of nineteenth-century North America needs to be linked with the histories of Europe and of the missionary movement; Christianity was in the ascendant in the United States, not least in its cities, at the very time of its decline in Europe, and the evangelization of the United States can count as the outstanding success of the missionary movement in the nineteenth century. (Certainly the other areas receiving immigrants from Europe, such as Australia, New Zealand, and South Africa, saw nothing like it.) And how can we understand the Pentecostal and charismatic movement — or should we say movements? — which represent such a prominent strain in the Christianity of so many parts of the world in the late twentieth century, without attention to their intercontinental and intercultural connections?

Another effect of a new vision might be to produce reflection on some of the less prosperous aspects of Christian history. One of these has already been mentioned; there are remarkably few examples of nomadic people who have become Christian and remained nomadic. Most of these few examples occurred in the high period of expansion of the ancient Church of the East. Yet Christian origins ultimately lie in the nomadic tradition of Abraham, and images of the nomadic life echo through the Christian Scriptures, in Christian iconography and rhetoric. Why has Islam, claiming in Abraham the same nomadic origins as Christianity, appealed to nomadic peoples when Christianity has offered them so little resonance? A vision that included such aspects of the Christian story might take note of the Native American and Australian Aboriginal Christian histories. For Western Catholics and Protestants alike, the Native American peoples were critically important, as the first non-Western peoples among whom they lived on close terms. Western missions cut their teeth on the American settlements. In the response to the Gospel among the "Praying Indians," the old Puritan John Eliot saw the ingathering of Israel, for how could the Native American peoples have preserved such knowledge of God unless it had come from revelation, such as the lost tribes of Israel might possess? Yet the history that unfolded in North America is frequently a depressing one. Widespread acceptance of the Christian faith does not seem to have saved either the Native American nations or their dignity, nor has it accorded them as yet any distinctive contribution to the world church, or any obvious sphere of leadership in it. The relative paucity of Native American movements offering a distinctively indigenous expression or appropriation of Christianity has been noted before. Christian symbolism stresses the power of powerlessness and the triumph of vulnerability. Christian history among the world's marginalized peoples may give space for Christian reflection on power relations.

Another dimension of the re-visioning process will be to place the study of Christianity firmly within the history of religions. I am not alluding here to the theological issues proper, to what is increasingly called the theology of religions, important as these are, but to a cluster of serious historical issues. The history of Christianity — of the whole Christian movement in all its paths and bypaths — is not the same exercise as church history, but it is a necessary companion discipline. It should be possible to give an account of events and processes in Christian history in terms and by methods analogous to those used for the history of Buddhism or Islam. And the comparisons may be illuminating, as Lamin Sanneh has shown with regard to the latter: how the distinctive character — what one might call the respective genius — of Christian and Islamic faith are revealed when manifested in what appear to be parallel situations. There are also questions of historical relationship which require exploration. What transpired in China between Nestorian Christians and Buddhists, Indians and Chinese, during those years in which both faiths were seeking to make their way in the Empire? What part did the missionary movement in India play in the formulation of modern Hinduism?

Above all, such study is necessary because the other religions form the sub-structure of Christianity. The study of Christianity must always take seriously the preexisting culture, since Christianity of its nature does so; and the religious elements cannot be separated out from the rest of the cultural mix.

Buddhist influences are always likely to shape the way that Christians from a Buddhist background embody Christianity. The primal religions that have always formed the background, at varying removes of time, of the majority of Christian believers are especially important for the understanding of Christian history, ancient and modern. African Christian history cannot be understood without reference to the old religions of Africa. Indeed, African Christianity can be studied either as an African chapter in Christian history or as the latest — the Christian — chapter in the history of African religion.

Finally, perhaps among the new visions there may be some that allow us to view Christian history as a whole. There are obvious gains from the process whereby specialists are now appointed for patristic, medieval, Reformation, and sundry forms of modern church history; but there have been losses too. There are fewer and fewer church historians *simpliciter* — fewer people charged with generalization about Christian history, and fewer and fewer prepared to undertake it. Yet the nature of Christian discourse requires that generalization should be a viable one; those engaged in the serious study of Christian history, with all due recognition of the specialist's reluctance to pronounce outside the field of specialization, have some responsibilities to it. Otherwise the task of the specialist in Reformation history is no different from that of the sixteenth-century specialist in the university history department.

It is easy to be misunderstood here. The church historian is, first and all the time, a historian, working by the rules of the historian's craft. The church historian cannot present bad history under the plea that it is good theology. Indeed, a principal function of history within a theological curriculum is to keep the theologians honest. But this does not mean that there is no contribution to be made to the understanding of the faith from reflection on its history. Church history — that is, history in a theological setting — is history written from the perspective of faith in the providence of God. The old church history sometimes interpreted this in terms of an implied definition of the "real" (that is, in effect, "our") church, and traced that church's origins, development, and distinctives, together with some indications of the perils, distortions, and malformations from which it had been rescued. The new church history will seek generalizations of a different kind. Some, as already noted, may be of the type made by historians of religions, viewing Christianity among the religions. Some may represent what one might call "systematic history." Some may have directly theological implications.

One field of generalization, for instance, might be the history of Christian expansion. That history has not been progressive, like that of Islamic expansion, but serial in nature. Christian history offers no picture of steady growth, of resistless triumph, but rather, as Latourette long ago indicated, of advance and recession. Hitherto, areas that have taken Islamic allegiance have, generally speaking — there are exceptions — retained it. Principal centers of Christian life — ancient Jerusalem in the first century, the Eastern Mediterranean lands after the seventh century, Western Europe more recently — cease to shine. Successively, the candlesticks are taken from their place. But the process of successive diminishment in centers of strength has not led to the disappearance of the Christian faith or the end of Christian witness, but to the appearance of new Christian centers elsewhere. No single place or culture owns the Christian faith or permanently dominates its expression. At different times, different peoples and places become its chief representatives. The rhetoric of some of our hymns about the triumphant host streaming out to conquer the world is more Islamic than Christian. Christian progress is never final, does not represent gains to be plotted on a map. The history of Christian expansion is serial; Christianity shows a tendency to wither in its heartlands and establish anew at or beyond the margins. It has vulnerability, a certain fragility, at its heart — the vulnerability perhaps of the Cross, and the fragility of the earthen vessel.

A similar process of reflection on Christian history as a whole might consider how that history is one of successive linguistic and cultural translation. The Incarnation itself is a great act of translation, God translated into humanity, the whole meaning of God expressed in human categories. But the incarnate Christ is not humanity generalized, but God expressed in the culture-specific terms of first-century Jewish Palestine. The only humanity we know and recognize as human is culture-specific. So the process of Christian expansion is the story of various re-translations of that original into other cultural media as Christ is received among people of different languages and cultures. The translational process is never complete (the very principle of translation is the principle of re-vision), and the translations themselves are all more or less imperfect; but their cumulation reveals an expanding of the Christian understanding of Christ, as the process of translation requires answers to questions posed by the way that different languages and worldviews are constructed. The first believers saw and preached Jesus as Messiah of Israel, and their convictions about him were entirely coherent in Jewish terms and consistent with their inherited understanding of Jewish experience and destiny. But when at Antioch some of them sought to introduce Jesus to Greek-speaking pagans, it was no use presenting him as Messiah; they needed a translation — not just a word (it was easy enough to produce a Greek word for Messiah), but a concept which would mean something to their neighbors. They chose to present Jesus as *Kyrios Iesus*. Jewish believers had certainly used the word Kyrios of Jesus among themselves ("God has made him both Lord and Christ"), but to use it among Greek pagans, who used the title of their cult divinities, was to take the Christ figure deep into a new realm of thought and to raise questions which it would not occur to a Jew to ask. Jewish believers could meaningfully indicate the relation of the Christ to the Lord of Hosts by a phrase like "at the right hand of Power." Such a phrase, with its anthropomorphic overtones, might simply obstruct the understanding of someone brought up in the Greek world. The relationship had ultimately to be expressed in terms of *ousia* and *hypostasis*. The long, painful quest involved thinking Christ into the categories and the methods of indigenous Greek intellectual discourse. But the process of asking Greek questions and obtaining Greek answers actually expanded the understanding of who Christ is, far beyond what could have arisen from the use of purely Jewish categories like Messiah — and this without in any way rendering "Messiah" or the other Jewish categories obsolete, or diluting the richness of their meaning. Subsequent cross-cultural encounters have produced similar expansions of understanding. It will be surprising if the present engagement of Christian faith with the ancient cultures of Africa and Asia does not do the same.

A further related reflection might relate to the inescapability of the theme of conversion in Christian history. Conversion means turning — turning toward Christ, opening to Him. It is essentially a change, not of substance, but of direction. One of the determining events in Christian history is the decision in Acts 15 not to apply to the Gentile believers in Jesus the tried and trusted method with which Jews had always welcomed Gentiles who desired to serve the God of Israel and join his people. Proselytes, having been baptized to symbolize the washing away of the dirt of the heathen world, were admitted into Israel with the sign of the covenant, the rite of circumcision. In an astonishing decision, the early church, utterly Jewish in its membership and outlook, abandoned the proselyte model for Gentile believers in Jesus. Despite the fact that the only way of devotion known to them was that of observant Jews; despite the fact that this lifestyle had been sanctified by the Lord himself and was currently followed by his brother, his chosen apostles, and all leaders of the church; it was agreed that Gentile believers in Jesus should not be required to follow that lifestyle. They were left to make a Christian lifestyle within Hellenistic society under the guidance of the Holy Spirit. They were not proselytes, but converts.

The difference between proselyte and convert is of fundamental importance. If the first Gentile believers had become proselytes, living exactly like the Jerusalem apostles, they might have become very devout believers, but they would have had a negligible effect on Hellenistic society. As converts, it was their task to turn Hellenistic social and family patterns, Hellenistic ways of thinking and coming to decisions, toward Christ, so that both Hellenistic social life and intellectual life were challenged, modified, confirmed, and altered, all from the inside. The experience transformed Hellenistic society, altered the direction of Greek thought (some would say rescued it), and changed the whole way in which Christianity was expressed.

Conversion is turning — not substituting a new element for the old or adding a new element to the old, but changing the direction of what is already there. The story of conversion discernible in the Greek world can be traced, in varying degrees, in every culture into which the faith has entered. Christianity takes the preexisting materials of thought and turns them toward Christ. As Origen says, the things of the heathen world are taken and from these are fashioned things for the worship and service of God.

The view at the beginning of the third millennium calls us to a reconception of the task of the Christian historian and offers a new vision to direct the study, teaching, and writing of Christian history. The task of research will be immeasurably expanded beyond what has ordinarily been in view, and vast unexplored sources are already at hand to support that research. The church historian's task will now need more than a simple, natural evolution from current practice. It will require a new breed of church historians with all the skills and virtues nourished in the older school but with a range of others as well, skills and virtues demanded by the new environment of Christianity in the southern continents. It is time for the re-commissioning of church historians.

— T W O —

THE CHANGING TASK
OF CHRISTIAN HISTORY

A View at the Onset of the Third Millennium

A. Mathias Mundadan, C.M.I.

The task of Christian history is in a state of great change. I will analyze the context, the historical and theological consciousness that seems to have emerged at this threshold of the third millennium. It is in the different facets of the world context, of this emerging human consciousness, that we see the signs of the times. These signs should guide us in our search for a new approach to recounting Christian history.

The context we are in today — the general consciousness that seems to be prevailing — may be viewed at several levels: the world context in general and the trends in secular historiography that have appeared recently; the Christian context and trends in Christian historiography and theology; the Indian context both general and Christian; and, finally, my own personal "context" or consciousness, resulting from my experience with studying, teaching, and writing Christian history.

The latter approach to church history that I have been following is one of encounter and assimilation, "encounter of the Christian message with the cultures and mutual assimilation" (Mundadan, 1997: 1–3). This approach has grown with the years, progressively shaped as it is by my early experience as a student of theology; by my later study of the traditions of the ancient (St. Thomas) Christians of India; by my research into the story of the meeting between the St. Thomas Christians and the Portuguese; by the inquiry into the connections of the Indian Christians with the East-Syrian Christians and their church; by the study and teaching of general church history based on some of the insights of Joseph Lortz (see 1962 and 1965); by the insights found in an article by A. Franzen in *Sacramentum Mundi* (1966: 366–73); by my study of the Hindu and Christian views of history (Mundadan, 1997: 49–81); by the overall influence of Vatican II, especially the "Constitution on the Church in the Modern World" (*Gaudium et spes*), the "Decree on Missions" (*Ad gentes*), the "Declaration on other Religions" (*Nostra aetate*), and to a limited extent the "Constitution on the Church" (*Lumen gentium*) and the "Constitution on Revelation" (*Dei verbum*); by my association from the early 1960s with the Church History Association of India (CHAI), especially its multivolume project, History of Christianity in India; and by my interest in the development of an Indian Christian theology (see Mundadan, 1998). A particular deciding factor in the shaping of my perspective is the ongoing controversy in the Syro-Malabar Church about the restoration or renewal of its liturgy and, consequently, the question of the identity of the St. Thomas Christians. Some of my recent readings in connection with the preparation of my book *Paths of Indian Theology* and for writing this essay (see Greinacher, 1994; Boff, 1991; Bühlmann, 1977; and Shenk, 1996) only served to confirm and even deepen this encounter perspective of history.

The History of Christianity as the History of Encounter

The history of Christianity is the history of the encounter of the gospel message of Jesus with different peoples and their ever-newer religious-cultural and sociopolitical contexts. It is the history of the impregnation of these contexts by the gospel, the assimilation of the cultures of the peoples by the gospel and that of the gospel by their cultures, and the history of the consequent changes in the Christian movement and of the cultures of the people. This idea began vaguely to dawn in my thoughts in the days of my graduate and postgraduate studies in theology. It was corroborated when I began teaching general church history or, more correctly, the history of Eastern and Western Christendom. I became more and more convinced that the formation of early Christianity both in the "East" and in the "West"[1] was the result of the encounter between the message of Jesus and the Greco-Roman world, a world which included the Jewish religion, the Greek culture, and the Roman state.

The spread of the Christian movement, that is, the process of evangelization, takes place not apart from the cultures but always arrives astride the existing

---

1. "West" is understood to be West Europe (and early North Africa) and "East" is East Europe, West Asia, Egypt, and Ethiopia.

cultural worldviews. The gospel is, of course, not identified with cultures but is identified in cultures. It cannot exist apart from a cultural expression. In Jesus' time and in the formative period of the church, the gospel got its first expression in the Semitic universe. Paul already had expressed it in the parameters of Hellenism and Judaism of the Diaspora. John used Greek patterns to express it. Christians of the first few centuries expressed the gospel in the Greco-Roman mold (Boff, 1991: 31). In West Asia, the Semitic expression continued and was further influenced by the Arabic, Syrian, Armenian, and Persian cultural patterns. In the West, the German and Slavic universe partially modified the Greco-Roman expressions. At the same time, in the Eastern half of the original Roman empire and in most of the Slavic countries, the Greco-Roman underwent some changes and emerged as the Byzantine or Slavic Oriental form.

During the Middle Ages the Greco-Roman matrix achieved a new synthesis under the impact of Aristotle's philosophy. It produced a theological outlook (not radically different from the early Greco-Roman), which was almost "absolutized" as the theology of the church and acted as the norm for evaluating cultures and religions of other peoples, even any developments in the West itself. It is this outlook that acted as the colonial *conquista* theology as Western Europe expanded to East Europe and Asia, Africa, and the Americas. It had the most devastating impact in the Americas, since it completely wiped out the Amerindian culture and people. It had also serious negative impacts in Asia and Africa, and in Western Christendom's relations with various groups that form Oriental Christendom. The church got so identified with this medieval cultural expression of the gospel that it was even named "the Christian era," "the Christian civilization," as if no other expression could be considered — hence the uneasiness that was experienced at the development of new philosophies and world visions as well as the discovery of new cultures and religions (in Asia, Africa, and the Americas).

My reflections on general church history raised basic questions regarding Christianity in India. Has the gospel had a real encounter with the Indian people, with their culture, with their worldview, with their religious outlook? Has the Christian gospel really touched the soul of India, and has an Indian Christian culture emerged? Did that happen in the ancient period? Did it happen later? Is it happening at present? If not, what were and what are the reasons? One could ask these questions regarding other peoples and their cultures in the so-called "Third World." The answer many theologians and historians of Christianity give is this: it is painfully realized that only a limited number of cultures have, so far, substantially absorbed and assimilated the Christian gospel and that was in the remote past, namely, the Jewish-Semitic, the Greco-Roman, and the Byzantine. For many centuries, the church has continued to live in that same Greco-Roman world. Many have considered that cultural encounter was the only possible encounter, and the pattern of synthesis was set once and for all. Wherever the Christian message reached, it was under the garb of that set pattern. No serious attempts since the early centuries have been made for a real meeting of the core of the Christian revelation with other cultures. Hence, historiography has generally been seen "as an eastward extension of western history" (CHAI, 1974: 89–90). Today's historians and those of the future have to squarely face this history of encounter and critically evaluate and charter their task accordingly.

The World Context

Some of the features of the present world context that I believe are outstanding will be highlighted now. One of the most important happenings of the second half of the twentieth century was that of "decolonization," understood as the emancipation of peoples who were subjected to colonial powers. This process is almost complete. Many independent nations have emerged with a new awakening of their cultural identity, a new self-consciousness. However, there exists a lingering concern about the phenomenon of "economic and technical colonialism," a "new imperialism." Even the word "globalization" is used in this context. The "Third World" theologians understand this term to mean "a phenomenon bound up with the growth and expansion of capitalism and the integration of national economies into its system." Globalization has grown, they think, from a mercantile slave-trading age and passed through an industrial colonial stage into a corporate new-imperialist stage that has resulted in unequal development and division of labor, "center-periphery" dependency, and a one-way flow of world wealth. "By engineering competitiveness, which is its dominant ideology, it creates polarization and leads to truncated markets." It is based on monopolies sustained by dominant nations (the "center"). The "Third World," understood as ex-colonies, is made to suffer. Such globalization undermines identity and effects the exclusion and marginalization of peoples and regions, and the "feminization" of poverty (EATWOT, 1997: 247; see Dussel, 1985).

Some radical thinkers have criticized the sociopolitical situation ensuing from the collapse of the Soviet Union with an unparalleled sharpness. They see a recolonizing attempt by the West after this collapse. Roger Garaudy calls it "the monotheism of market," while for Sebastian Kappen it is "the monotheism of the capital." The latter says that the old adage "No salvation outside the church" has given way to "No salvation outside the market."

> To propagate this message, the centers of capitalism are sending out missionaries by the thousands to the less industrialized countries of Asia and Africa that are not yet fully integrated into the "saving" sphere of the market. The whole venture has been aptly called "re-colonization."
>
> The neo-colonialists believe that their success is guaranteed because they have an ultimate secular sanction in the nuclear weapons they have accumulated. For the so-called developing nation the only option is between consumerism utopia or nuclear devastation. (Kappen, 1995: 2)

Kappen feels that a "still greater guarantor of re-colonization is the Christian Ungod, distinct from the Divine whom Jesus met." This situation, whether it is dismal or not, is a great challenge for Christian history.

A second phenomenon is what a number of thinkers call the emergence of a "new epoch." Jean Leclerque claims that between the end of World War II and the sixties a mutation occurred on a global basis, ushering in a new stage in the forward movement of the historical process. This was brought about by the development of atomic energy, increased communications, and the many forces at work through centuries that led to the convergence of cultures. It has resulted in the encounter of world religions and the convergence of the great traditions of spirituality (one may perhaps add secular ideologies). Leclerque's notion could be usefully compared with Teilhard's concept of "planetization" and the radical change which the latter claims has occurred over the last century, shifting the forces from divergence to convergence in the sphere of the human community (Cousins, 1979: 142). The main thrust of this theory is that a new awakening has happened, a movement toward intercultural, interreligious, inter-ideology relations in the world, a mutual positive encounter, and a more positive universal vision. To this may be added what some eco-friendly thinkers postulate. They speak of the end of the "Cenozoic" age (sixty-five million years ago to the present, marked by the rapid evolution of mammals, birds, grasses, shrubs, and high flowering plants) and the beginning of the "ecozoic" age. A spirituality of "exodus," according to these thinkers, is the need of the day (see Berry, 1987). Both of these phenomena, the "new epoch" and the "ecozoic" age, deserve the serious attention of Christian historians.

Modern Historiography

Historical critics observe an expansion and fragmentation of the universe of history: the field of history has expanded and each category has splintered into newer and newer branches. Hence, a need is felt for orientation and for something of a possible synthesis, although the task is a difficult one. We hear about the "new history" (*la nouvelle histoire*), which had its origin in France ("made in France," like *la nouvelle vogue* and *le nouveau roman,* not to mention *la nouvelle cuisine!*). Started perhaps very early, its recent expression may be found in the *Annales* school founded in 1929 by Lucien Febvre and Marc Bloch. Fernand Braudel carried its scope to the present dimensions. It claims to deal with new problems, new approaches, new objects and aims at a "total history" (*histoire totale*).[2]

Peter Burke enumerates seven points of contrast between the old/traditional or the nineteenth-century "Rankean" model and the "new" models. While the former is concerned with politics, the latter are concerned virtually with every human activity, the philosophical foundation of which is that reality is culturally or socially constituted. Traditional history is essentially a narrative of events, but the new history focuses on the analysis of structures. If the old history is a view "from above" (great deeds of great men, and so on), the new is "history from below" (concerned with views of ordinary people and with their experience of social change). History from below points to the limitation of "Rankean" "documented" history and uses a greater variety of evidence, a greater variety of human activities (visual, oral, statistical, and so on). The old history's concern for historical explanation is criticized by the new historians because the former fails to answer the variety of questions of historians which are often concerned with collective movements as well as individual actions, with trends as well as events. The new historians consider the old school's regard for objective history as an unrealistic ideal because particular points of view, cultural relativism, the network of conventions, schemata, and stereotypes vary from culture to culture. Both old and generally new historians are professionals. However, the concern of the latter for the whole range of human activity leads them to be interdisciplinary: they insist on learning from and collaborating with social anthropologists, economists, literary critics, psychologists, sociologists, and so on.

---

2. This "alternative" history has a reasonably long ancestry. What is new is that its pioneers are now extremely numerous and they refuse to be marginalized.

According to Burke, decolonization and feminism are two movements which have obviously had a great impact on recent historical writing. In the future, the ecological movement is likely to have an increasing influence on history as in theology and ideology. A wide notion of culture (not merely high art, literature, music, and so on) is central to the new approach to history. However, there are a number of problems that were posed in connection with the ideals of the new history: the meaning of "popular culture," of "everyday life" (*la vie quotidienne, Alltagsgeschichte*), the nature of sources, of methods, of explanation, and so on. Burke asks whether the two approaches coexist and how to coordinate the expansion and fragmentation. He proposes a solution "summed up into two opposite points, complementary rather than contra- dictory." Proliferation of sub-disciplines is virtually inevitable. It has many advantages: it adds to human knowledge and encourages more rigorous methods and more professional standards. At the same time, there are also some disad- vantages, as is evident from the problems enumerated above. Communication between disciplines or sub-disciplines is one way of keeping the disadvan- tages at a minimum. There are encouraging signs of rapprochement, if not of synthesis.

In the spurt of newfound enthusiasm for the "new history," independence from or even opposition to the old became very strong. "Micro-history" and the history of "everyday life" were reactions against the study of grand social trends, a society without a human face. Now reaction against this reaction is slowly emerging. Historians of popular culture are open to the changing re- lations between the high and the low, to the interaction of popular culture and the culture of the educated people (see Gurevich, 1988). The history of women now shows concern for gender relations in general and the historical construction of masculinity as well as femininity (for example, "Why Gender and History?" in *Gender and History,* 1989: 1–6). Opposition between events and structures is being replaced by interrelationship, and a few historians are ex- perimenting with narrative forms of analysis and analytical forms of narratives. Most important of all is the fact that the long-standing opposition between political and nonpolitical historians is finally dissolving. G. M. Trevelyan's no- torious definition of social history as "history with the politics left out" is now rejected. Concern for social elements in politics and political elements in society is on the increase. Political histories no longer confine themselves to high politics, to leaders, to the *élite,* but are prepared to discuss sociology of elections and "the republic in the village" (see Agulhon, 1982). They are prepared to examine "political cultures," the assumptions about politics forming part of everyday life but differing from one period or region to another. Society and culture are now viewed as arenas for decision making, and political histories discuss "the politics of the family" and "the politics of language."

The concept "culture" in its wide, anthropological sense may serve as "a possible basis" for the reintegration of different approaches to history. We are still a long way from the "total history" (*histoire totale*) advocated by Braudel. Indeed it would be unrealistic to believe that the goal could ever be attained, but a few more steps have been taken toward it (see Burke, 1991).

A word about a particular branch of history that some historians have called "overseas history" may be relevant here. It was once "colonial history" and in the British context has been given a new name, "Imperial and Commonwealth history." Perhaps a more neutral term is "Third World" history (generally understood as history of Africa, Asia, and Latin America). It has its own problems, especially regarding a proper definition. What exactly is the connotation of these various titles? Is it the history of the former colonies and their relation with the colonizing nations during the colonial period, or is it a more comprehensive history of these nations before and during the post-colonial era? It seems the meaning has undergone a great evolution since 1945, a definite year in the decolonization process. It is becoming more and more comprehensive and also Africa-, Asia-, and Latin America–centered rather than Europe-centered. For the evolution of these overseas or Third World histories, the influence of the *Annales* school is significant. Hank Wesseling considers the unique phenomenon of the development of an African, Asian, or Latin American history to be natural and necessary, although their connection with Europe since 1500 poses a problem. The rise of the "American empire" has produced some rethinking. He derives a few conclusions: The distinctiveness between the autonomous history of Asia and Africa and the history of European expansion needs to be kept. African and Asian histories have proved their right to existence, just like European and American histories; for the last five centuries or so, the histories of various parts have been interconnected and various civilizations have influenced one another.

Wesseling identifies two approaches or two ways of dealing with the problem of world history — one labeled as "historical micro-sociology" and the other more traditional. The former is a social science approach, and its aim is to learn more about social process in general. The latter is more interested in the differences between various developments and the uniqueness of certain events than in their similarities. Both approaches are characterized by a strong desire to transcend traditional boundaries, particular views, and nationalist bias. The goal of both, according to Wesseling, is to make the specific Western discipline of history applicable to world history (1991: 67–92).

The Christian Context and the Emerging Pattern of Christian Historiography

I have already referred to what many believe to be a new epoch in human history. Karl Rahner considers that the arrival of this epoch coincides with the Second Vatican Council. According to him, the Council is a caesura in church history of "a quality which is paralleled only by the opening up of the Jewish Jesus community to the Gentiles or to the sphere of Western culture."

> It means that the transition from one historical and theological situation into an essentially new one happened only once before in the history of Christianity and is now set to occur for the second time in the transition from the Christianity of Europe (with its American appendage) to an actual world religion. (Rahner, 1981: 82–84)

Thus the Second Vatican Council represents a sudden and generally unexpected beginning of a new epoch in Christian history, a third period — the first being that of the Judeo-Christianity which lasted only a short while, and the second, the long nineteen hundred years of Hellenism and European culture and civilization (ibid.: 82–84).

Purely in phenomenological terms, this means the changed consciousness of the modern *quantity* of Christianity, not confined to the Mediterranean world, nor to Europe, but the whole world, especially the so-called "Third World" where, according to Walbert Bühlmann (1977), by A.D. 2000 70 percent of the Catholic (of course, Christian) population is expected to live. However, Rahner's argument is a theological one. For him, the epoch signifies a stopping place in the calculation of time, not a transition from one period to another. It denotes that everything that had shaped the preceding time comes to a standstill, is finally superseded, and something unprecedented, something totally new begins. Paul's victory at the Jerusalem Council represents such an epoch-making event. From Paul to Vatican II, that is, for nineteen hundred years, the history of theology moved in relative continuity. Vatican II brought about a revolution of theology, a revolution of Catholic identity (Greinacher, 1994: 4f; see also Rahner, 1981). Archbishop John R. Quinn seems to agree with this view when he says that the "new situation" is comparable to the situation that confronted the primitive church when it abandoned the requirement of the Mosaic Law and embraced the mission to the Gentiles. The action required immense courage, vision, and sacrifice. It was an uncharted path, a major change. There were grave reasons for keeping the Mosaic Law, not least of which was the fact that our Lord himself observed it. Yet, trusting in the Holy Spirit, the Apostles made that momentous decision. The decision required by the new situation will be exacting and costly (1997: 59). Raimon Panikkar, whom many look to as a "mutational man," is convinced that humanity is facing a mutation, a crisis, and the usual categories will help no more. A new council, a Jerusalem II, is the need of the day (1996: 25).

I wonder whether all would accept fully the views of Rahner and Panikkar. However, everybody will agree with what Wilbert Shenk says: "The changed reality [which he had analyzed at some length] ... means that every form and ethos of the Church has been substantially transformed as the result of its dispersion 'to the uttermost parts of the world'" (1996: 54). There would also be no difficulty in agreeing with the idea that the majority church is already or soon going to be in the southern hemisphere, the "Third World."

A word about the "Third Church" or churches of the "Third World" is in order here. Bühlmann considers that one of the discoveries of the Second Vatican Council is the "local church" (1977: 270–96). In the early church, local churches had their particular personality. St. Paul's missionary method helped this process. He refrained from tutoring the local churches he had established, still more from dominating them. This helped them to understand themselves to be one church of the saints and the elect (Rom. 1:7, 1 Cor. 1:2, and so on). But because of their autonomy, they developed particular characteristics. The first Christian communities were able to find spontaneous pragmatic solutions in close relationship with the environment. Very soon, various churches with their own liturgies, theologies, and administration emerged. Each of these churches revealed something of the riches and fullness of God; only the sum of them enabled the crown to shine forth in full glory. Despite some centralizing and even domineering tendencies of the "metropolitan" churches, the principle of the local church remained more or less the model of missionary activity for the first millennium. It is the modern missionary system, the mission model from the age of "discovery," that brought about a radical change. Missionary activity ceased to be a matter of short stay only; it became colonization. In the mission territory, what ought to have been the local church was committed to the rule of a group of foreign missionaries and became faceless, a passive community, a kind of dependency of the "mother church," a scaled-down version of the European church.

Leonardo Boff (1991: 104–7) considers even the "peaceful evangelization" of Las Casas was not peaceful enough. It violated the religious sentiments of the Aztecs. The religions of the native went unacknowledged. It was tantamount to destroying the heart of their culture, because religion was the heart of their culture. And to destroy the heart of culture meant the cultural death of a people. All this was a consequence of the narrow Christian dogmatism of those days. It produced a Christianity without cultural roots, an incorporation of the natives into the Iberian universe, into a single, stereotyped European Christendom. The historical opportunity to create a Christianity culturally distinct from the Western form was lost.

Today this situation has changed. Decolonization and the consequent emancipation spirit have brought about a new consciousness. The deep consciousness of being a local church finds emphatic expression in various circles of the Third World church. A concrete example is the Puebla Statement, no. 446:

> It is the Gospel, fleshed out in our peoples, that has brought them together to form the original cultural and historical entity known as Latin America. And this ideology is glowingly reflected on the *mestizo* countenance of Mary of Guadalupe, who appeared at the start of the evangelization process. (Eagleson and Scharper, 1979: 184–85)

The new evangelization will be new only if it creates a Christianity of communities and not a society of Christendom, massive, with its relationships anonymous, asymmetrical, and marked by a rigid division of functions in the church.

Among the theologians and historians of the Third World, the idea of "center-periphery" continues. It may be a hangover from the colonial era, but persisting still in the context of "neo-imperialism" and globalization which undermine the identity of people, impose exclusivism and marginalization on them; and discriminate against gender, race, culture, and religion. They postulate a counterbalancing, which should emerge from true interdependence and interaction, and recognition of diversity and difference (of gender, race, religion, and ethnic and cultural realities). The principles of counterbalancing are: reverence for "Mother Earth," opting for the poor (reject policies and moves that hurt people and exclude or deny them participation), and sustainable development (not destructive of resources, spiritualities, peoples, and our common future); interrelation of universalities and particularities (articulation of macro-micro realities: what happens at local levels may require global action and reflection, and vice versa); new paradigms: imagination, affectivity, and symbolic action becoming important; poverty, gender, race, ethnicity, religion, and culture to remain permanent elements in our theory and practice; and solidarity as an ethical principle of interaction based on mutuality and equalization of power. They see the revolts in America, Vietnam, the Philippines, India, South Africa, Nigeria, Cuba, Angola, and so on as links in a long chain of searching for a new world. The biblical "new heaven and new earth," the sabbatical year, Jubilee, Jesus' search for a new earth, and the "Basileia of God" are all to be seen in this light. Religious pluralism and the reality of the poor and the marginalized people are challenges for a prophetic theology and a prophetic history. They want to retain the term "Third World" as signifying "social, economic, political, religious, and cultural forces which render our people expendable." So also they want to keep the expression "center-periphery" (EATWOT, 1997: 247–57).

The center-periphery idea existed both in the society and in the church much before the fifteenth/sixteenth century. But the Third World theologians and historians mean by it the phenomenon that emerged from the fifteenth/sixteenth century and was accentuated in 1870. "Center" refers to the political power, accumulation of economic capital, technical progress, ideological and cultural hegemony, and the pole of religious expansion (Christian evangelization). And "periphery" refers to the receiving end. Enrique Dussel, speaking of the evangelization in the "Periphery" (fifteenth to twentieth centuries), divides it into five cycles (that is, the last five of eight or nine cycles of evangelization in general, from the first to the twentieth centuries). The end of the process of the last cycle is marked by the emergence of a new concept of evangelization from the 1960s on. In this cycle, there are no more mission lands, but only the territory of the churches and domestic evangelization. This phase is noted for the "first emancipation," the social phenomenon and crisis of capitalism, and the "second emancipation," liberation, organization, and growth. Here the historian's attention must turn to three stages of evangelization in the "periphery," prior to colonial invasion, equivocal reception of the gospel under colonial invasion, and organization and growth that emerged with decolonization and emancipation (1985: 110–30).

Another important factor that concerns Christian thinkers today is the ecological crisis. In the Christian context, the crisis means giving up "that primordial, inherent relationship" between the human and the divine — the exaltation of the human as a spiritual being to the exclusion of the spiritual dimension of the created world as a whole. Redemption is thought of as some kind of out-of-this-world liberation experienced as "transcendencies" (transcendent deity, transcendent human, transcendent redemption, transcendent mind, and transcendent technology). Thomas Berry says that this is all the result of a discipline of the outside as is prevalent in the West, which promotes control of the very structure and functioning of the natural world. What is needed is a discipline from within, which characterizes people of the East and the South. These thinkers speak of the end of the "Cenozoic" age and the beginning of the "ecozoic" age, as referred to earlier. Hence there is need for a new spirituality, a spirituality of "exodus" from anthropocentrism to biocentrism and geocentrism, from "democracy" to "biocracy," which is the promised land (see Berry, 1987).

These various aspects of today's Christian context, whether we agree with the views expressed by different groups of thinkers or not, are challenges for Christian historians of today and tomorrow. Wilbert Shenk (1996: 50–53) has made a review of the emerging Christian historiography, especially against the mission context in Africa. The general practice in the West was to write history from the European "metropolitan" viewpoint that tended to neglect the changed reality of the church. There are signs now of moving beyond this conventional assumption that what happened in the West is universally normative for Christian history. There is increasing criticism of this assumption. Fresh approaches, the breaking down of parochialism, and reevaluation of the missionary process are on the increase. Shenk concentrates on these fresh approaches in histories and missiological studies of African Christianity produced by Western writers like King Fairbank, Andrew Porter, Maurice Leenhardt, Bengt Sunkler, Ronald Oliver, F. B. Welbourn, John V. Taylor, Andrew Walls, Richard Gray, and others. He also analyzes the African viewpoint represented by the studies of African writers like Ekechi, Tasie, and especially Ajayi and Ayandele. The last two writers mentioned, in their essay "Writing African Church History," have argued provocatively, "A bitter pill which the majority of writers on Christianity and missionary activities should swallow is that they have not been writing African Church History." Shenk also briefly refers to the initiative taken in India by CHAI to write a new history of Christianity in India and by CEHILA in Latin America, and also to ecumenical efforts undertaken by the Working Commission on Church History of EATWOT (Ecumenical Association of Third World Theologians).

The Indian Context

Here, my typical case for study is that of India. It may provide us with a model for writing Christian history in the third millennium, especially the Christian history of Asia, and to some extent other countries of the Third World, or even for a global Christian history. In India, Christian thinkers, theologians, missiologists, and historians are seriously confronted with the problem of the encounter of the gospel message with culture — with the problem of the gospel's impregnation of culture in its various dimensions and facets. Consider some of the questions alluded to at the beginning of this chapter, questions that I, myself, was forced to ask.

The ancient Christians of India had not developed an articulate theology or historical vision of their own, due mainly to two factors: their dependence on a church (the East-Syrian church) foreign and away from the home environment and their easy accommodation to the caste system and an aristocratic ethos. They had, however, developed a vision and a lifestyle of their own which somehow or other was congenial to the ground realities of their sociocultural and religious milieu. It was a vision and life of coexistence and of respect for other faiths. Had this genuine Indian Christian vision developed and continued, the Indian church would have been different. It was the East-Syrian model of theology and praxis in early times and the Western *conquista* model in later centuries that seem to have prevented a proper development of that genuine Indian Christian outlook. The particular situation in which the St. Thomas Christians find themselves is one important element of the Christian context in India. I shall now refer to the Christian awakening which started with the general national movement in the nineteenth century and which continues even today.

To the national stirrings in the nineteenth century and early twentieth, the Christian churches were rather cool and indifferent, if not outright hostile. The official reaction to the genuine efforts of a loyal Catholic lay theologian, as was Brahmabandab Upadhyaya, was one of contempt, derision, and hostility. If the Indian churches continue to bear a foreign garb and if the gospel message has not succeeded in impregnating the culture of India, the main responsibility rests with the official attitude of the churches and the hostile actions of the missionaries against the life and vision of ancient Christians in India, against such movements as those of de Nobili, Brahmabandab, and other pioneering spirits. Of course, slowly a change has set in during the last century, but its wind has yet to take stronger and swifter wings under official initiative.

It was some Renaissance Hindus of the last century like Raja Ram Mohan Roy, K. C. Sen, and others who started, many years after the deplorable death of the de Nobili experiment, a new era of Hinduism encountering Christianity or the Christian gospel. Then there arose a galaxy of Indian Christian writers, including the young "Hindu-Christian" Brahmabandab who, deeply rooted in the culture and religion of India, took over and gave a new impetus for a genuine encounter of the gospel message with the newly awakened self-awareness of Indian culture and religion. Some continuity was kept up until the middle of the twentieth century, particularly by eminent Indian Protestant thinkers and sages. By this time, a few European scholars and spiritual men arrived in India, in search of the soul of India. They were instrumental in promoting a deeper theological-spiritual encounter of the message of Jesus and the Indian religious core. At the same time, a new generation of Indian theologians and spiritual contemplatives came forward to give a further push to the movement and bring about a tremendous momentum to it (see Mundadan, 1998).

It seems that it was the recognition of a situation like this prevailing in the second half of the twentieth century that urged theologians like Karl Rahner and Raimon Panikkar to speak of a new epoch. This epoch is comparable to the one when Judaic Christianity was challenged by the Gentile world in the first century itself. This encounter with the Greco-Roman implied first a confrontation followed by persecution and then an accommodation. During the confrontation period, the church was of the poor and the marginalized. But this church of the poor soon vanished, and accommodation led to the development of a state church, a "Christendom." Today the church is forced to face the realities of some of the highly developed cultures of Asia, as well as the less developed cultures of both Asia and Africa, and particularly the less developed economies of the Third World, the traumatic experience of thousands of millions of poor, illiterate groups of people all over the world. The challenges for the church today are on one side the living cultures and religions of the newly awakened peoples that demand an encounter similar to the one in the Greco-Roman world; on the other side, the poverty of the people calls for *diakonia,* service.

Today's challenges in India are many. There is first of all the age-old philosophical wisdom of India, which is comparable to or even superior to the ancient wisdom of the Greeks. Then there is the deep religious experience of the Indian people, with the popular, religious-contemplative, and religious-philosophical expressions of it. There are the secular ideologies, in their liberal modern, moderate socialist, and more radical Marxist forms, concerned with the liberation of the people from various forms of bondage (poverty, illiteracy, caste and class discrimination, class domination, and ecological imbalance), and with their all-round progress. Many Indian thinkers (Indians as well as non-Indians doing theology and history in the Indian context) are seriously responding to the challenges these manifold aspects have revealed, from as genuine an understanding as possible of the message of Jesus found in the gospel. The emphasis of one thinker or a group of thinkers may differ from another. Hence, the wide variety of approaches, but they are not mutually exclusive or separate. They are interrelated, and the different paths have a fundamental unity. Pluralism of views is there, but these views are not contradictory; they are complementary. The ultimate concern is the same, to discover today's India in the light of Jesus' gospel message. This discovery involves looking back to the cultural and spiritual past which is not the story of a smooth, unopposed growth, but also of protests and oppositions that have helped reevaluation and regeneration, and a looking forward to the emergence of a model secular India sensitive to people's needs and nature's delicate environment.

These thinkers proceed from certain presuppositions and convictions like the following. The liberating saving power of Jesus Christ was already in India and is at work in India today, in the philosophical-religious and religious-contemplative experiences of her people. It is active in the secular ideologies that had their antecedents in the religious protests, such as the Buddhist movements in ancient times and the *Bhakti* movement of the Middle Ages. It is critically present in the modern secular movements of Pandit Nehru, Jaya Prakash Narain, and others, and in the social movements as represented by Socialists and Marxists. It is not absent even in some of the subversive movements, such as those of the Naxalites. The means they use may be questionable; their approach to the divine may not be acceptable, but the genuine concern of all these movements is humanization and integral liberation that in Christian terms is salvation-redemption, the meaning of the Cross and resurrection (Mundadan, 1998: ch. 5).

Indian Historiography

Since 1945, significant advances were made in the general historiography in India. The field expanded significantly, both in quantity and quality. A number of scientific and professional periodicals came into existence, which opened up studies on various aspects of Indian history. Also, the field got enormously diversified: a variety of subject matter, the kinds of research questions, and the kinds of sources and techniques used. A great novelty was the recognition of history as a social science, the use of social science theory for formulating research questions, and the use of social science techniques for analyzing sources. Another interesting development was that some historians of India from the

academy, both Christians and others, wrote important pieces on Christians and
Christianity in India. All of them, with rare exceptions, wrote from the Indian
rather than from the Christian point of view. The result, says Webster, was
more academic than churchly; the aims and methods were shaped more by the
academy or university than the church (1978: 110–48).

Indian historians are convinced that change is the "undeniable law of life,
and history is a pursuit that attempts to grasp the course of change." Much
change has come over the last thirty or fifty years and has transformed Indian historiography beyond recognition. It has achieved a share of success in
effecting a paradigm shift in analysis and interpretation. A qualitative change
started with the onset of nationalism. There is a concentration on social history, necessitated as it is by the recognition that society in present-day India
carries divisions, classes, and class or caste conflicts. Need is felt for writing
history from the Marxist point of view just as for any other point of view. The
nineteenth-century approach to history is rejected; the historians have shifted
their interests from personalities to social and economic trends.

Despite the advance made by post-colonial Indian historiography, the need
to explore new areas and refine existing methodologies remains. No other theme
in modern Indian historiography evoked so much interest, even passion, as the
complex manner in which Indians became conscious of their nationhood and
organized themselves to oppose and overthrow colonial rule. In the historiography of nationalism itself, different strands have emerged. The relationship
between colonialism and nationalism is fundamental. There are two different
ideological approaches to the problem of this relationship: the liberal view that
colonialism and nationalism are complementary and the critical view which
divorces the two. The Marxists relate the internal class struggles and the anti-
colonial movement. The major weakness of this approach is the relative neglect
of caste and culture. Culture transcended such limits to create the worldview
of people. This was a terrain in which modernity articulated and negotiated,
and the cultural common sense of people was reformulated. Marxists fail to
give adequate response to this fact. The recent renewal of the cognizance of
the cultural context of nationalism and the significance of cultural struggles in
the making of national consciousness is particularly important in the context
of a culturalist interpretation of nationalism advanced by Hindu communalists
and postmodern radicals.

The subaltern group has come forward to write history from below. The
approach is welcome, but some historians have felt that to create a "new"
world by completely negating the old is prone to produce a myopic view. And

some of the essays of the subaltern historians, they fear, can even help to bring a comeback of colonial and communal histories through the "radical" back door.

New trends in Indian historiography gradually discard the periodization into Hindu, Muslim, British, or the equivalent Ancient, Medieval, and Modern. Accordingly, the line of demarcation has to be made on the basis of fundamental social changes, which do not necessarily coincide with invasions, conquests, and dynastic changes. Regional history sometimes tends toward regional chauvinism. If this is avoided and if placed in perspective, regional history can usefully modulate the generalization about historical change on a national level and will demonstrate that there is a multiplicity of histories, even of early India, which have to be co-related. When there are various perspectives on the same event, the historian has to be aware of this variance, both in looking for evidence and in interpreting it. The greater the contention, the more there will be a honing of generalizations. The survival of history as a discipline depends as much on theoretical rigor as on historical data.

Some Pakistani historians see the history of "Muslims in India" as a struggle for a separate national right from A.D. 712, when Mohammad ibn Qasim entered Sind. Against this, some Indian historians characterize the entire period from circa 1200 onward to be one of foreign rule. The mainstream historians, however, have a much broader and critical view. They show a greater readiness to study the factors of change and stagnation and to identify various internal economic, social, and ideological contradictions. Historians are making a new assessment of Medieval India, and there is a growing criticism of nationalist and Marxist historiography of precolonial India. There are definite signs of the tendency that the given histories are not taken in trust (see Habib, Panikkar, and Thapar, 1997).

Indian Christian Context and Historiography

John C. B. Webster has written an article (1978), which, in the words of Wilbert Shenk, is "a masterly overview of ecclesiastical historiography in India." It has, however, a few limitations; it is restricted to the 150 years before the CHAI history project was launched in the 1970s, although a reference was made to the account of Michael Geddes (1694) on the Church of Malabar (close of the seventeenth century), and indirectly to the *Jornada* of Gouvea (1606), which is Geddes's source. Admittedly, Webster's survey and analysis is on histories written in English, not in other European languages or in

Indian languages. There are histories in other European languages, especially
in Portuguese in the sixteenth century, and also in Indian languages, especially
in Malayalam.

Here reference may be made to the historical consciousness of the ancient (St. Thomas) Christians of India as it is manifested in some Portuguese
documents or some other later records. Some of the salient features of their
historical consciousness are the following: Theirs was an Indian church founded
by the Apostle Thomas at the very beginning of the Christian era. They had
lived the same social-cultural life as their Hindu brethren. They lived in a very
cordial relationship with the latter and respected their faith and religious praxis.
Their church, founded by one of the apostles, was an individual church, which
had established an early relation with the East-Syrian church, and because of
that connection had received certain elements of the East-Syrian tradition of
worship and church order. They were part of the universal Church of Christ
and evinced solidarity with all Christians from wherever they came (from the
sixteenth century onward, mainly from the West). They respected the different
customs and usage of the foreign Christians and expected the latter to respect
those of the Indian Christians, the St. Thomas Christians. These features made
up their identity and selfhood. They would resist any encroachment upon this
identity and selfhood. Their turbulent history from the early sixteenth century to the nineteenth and to some extent up to the present is the story of
their protest against attempts at such encroachments on the part of foreigners:
Western missionaries as well as Syrian churches.

In the sixteenth century, the Portuguese started recording the history of
Indian Christianity. Gouvea's *Jornada*, composed at the turn of the seventeenth
century and published together with the acts and decrees of the so-called Synod
of Diamper (Udayamperur), and an account by Francis Ros, S.J., written about
1604 (never published), are perhaps the earliest systematic "histories" of the
ancient period of Christianity in India. While Gouvea the Augustinian gloated
over the "good work" carried out by his *confrère* Archbishop Meneses among
the St. Thomas Christians, Ros, the Jesuit, highlighted the "success story" of
the Jesuits. Two general mission histories were composed after this: one by the
Franciscan Paulo Trindade, written in the beginning of the seventeenth century
(1962–67), and the other by the Jesuit Francisco de Souza, written at the
turn of the eighteenth century and published in 1710. Trindade's is a story of
double triumph: the glorious achievements of the Franciscans in the East and
the conquest (*Conquista Espiritual*) of the religion and territories of the people
of the East by Christians of the West. It covers the whole of the sixteenth

century and early seventeenth century. Trindade wrote to defend the missionary activities of the Franciscans against criticisms by other missionaries, especially the Jesuits. He wrote, stressing the elements that impressed his contemporaries: miracles, number of converts, and the reputation that the Franciscans enjoyed in high places. "He was not a man to let a happening bearing the miraculous be unheralded if he could possibly help it" (Meersman, 1963: 480).

De Souza's history is also one of triumph and conquest (*Oriente Conquistado* — "The East Won over to Christ by the Jesuits"). The extant two volumes of this history cover the mission of the Jesuits from 1542 to 1585. A third volume is known to have been written, but has not yet been traced (Correia-Afonso, 1969: 124). De Souza is much less inclined than Trindade to "devout partiality," more sober on the miraculous. He is critical of exaggerations in favor of the Society of Jesus. His critical sense and discrimination have won for him recognition as a trustworthy historian. However, he is very sparing in giving attention to the work of non-Jesuit missionaries. He claims that the lands newly discovered by the Portuguese lay virtually untouched. It is this vast, almost virgin field that Francis Xavier, "the Apostle of India," and his fellow Jesuits, those brave soldiers of Christ, came and embarked on their arduous mission. De Souza is as eloquent as Trindade when he enumerates the various achievements of the Jesuit "soldiers." Like the Franciscan historian, the Jesuit historian also regards the Portuguese not only as soldiers of the sovereign of Portugal but also of Christ, who gave them victory because they took arms for his glory. When the Portuguese were engaged in a battle in Malacca, Xavier was praying and saw in a vision the impending victory. The approach of both Trindade and De Souza is the narrow, *conquista* ideology of the Western missionaries (Mundadan, 1997: 110–32). There were a number of other histories, but they are much less comprehensive than the above two. All these were "mission histories," written from the missionary point of view; they were success stories, *conquista* stories, permeated with the Western *conquista* mentality and with what one might call "the *conquista* theology" (Mundadan, 1998: ch. 2).

At the end of the seventeenth century, Michael Geddes wrote his *History of the Church of Malabar*, based, as mentioned above, on *Jornada* of Gouvea. In it there is a faithful English translation of the decrees of the "Synod of Diamper." He was writing at a time when no Protestant mission had been started, and yet he was very apologetic and came out strongly against the "Popists," the Catholic missionaries who, he alleged, tormented the St. Thomas Christians whose doctrinal tenets were, in his opinion, more in agreement with the Anglican tenets than the "Popish" or Roman tenets. In the eighteenth century, two histories appeared, one by La Croze (Protestant, 1724) and the other by Paulinus (Catholic, 1794). The stories of the first Indian bishop of the Latin rite, Matteo de Castro Mahalo (seventeenth century), and Padre Caetano Vittorino de Faria (eighteenth century; see Mundadan, 1984), both nationalists who rebelled against the Portuguese Padroado system and worked for the indigenization of the Indian hierarchy, are recorded in various Portuguese sources. In the last quarter of the eighteenth century, an exceptional book was written in incisive Malayalam, in the form of a travelogue, but with penetrative anti-missionary historical reflections, evincing strong national sentiments, by a St. Thomas Christian priest from Kerala, Cathenar Thomas Paremmakkal (1971). As it contained sharp and poignant attacks on the Carmelite missionaries who were at the helm of affairs over the Catholic St. Thomas Christians at that time, they even forbade its reading by the people.

Webster, in his article referred to above, critically analyzes some general histories of Christianity in India: histories of James Hough (1824–60), John Kaye (1859), M. A. Sherring (1875), and Julius Richter (1906/1908). These histories were composed by Protestants and carry on the anti-Catholic apologetics that Geddes had started at the end of the seventeenth century. In the twentieth century, there was change in various respects. Especially, we note a change in perspective. Webster cites the examples of histories of Rajaiah D. Paul (1952) and P. Thomas (1954). While the emphasis of the former is on the history of the Indian church, that of the latter is on the history of the Christian community. In the same century, there were four or five histories of the St. Thomas Christians (two by St. Thomas Christians themselves[3] and two or three by Europeans[4]). In the former, the anti-Western emphasis and also to some extent the Catholic-Orthodox polemics find their place.

From the 1920s onward a good deal of the original sources, especially of Portuguese sources of mission enterprises in India, began to be published under the initiatives of such writers as George Schurhammer, Josef Wicki, Antonio da Silva-Rego, and others. Histories based on these documents also began to appear by the middle of the century. From the fifties onward, Indian Catholic clerical students started taking special training in church history at the Gregorian University, Rome, and some other universities. The early research was on the sixteenth and seventeenth centuries, based mostly on original Portuguese

---

3. Bernard of St. Thomas, TOCD, and Z. M. Parett.
4. Eugene Cardinal Tisserant and L. W. Brown.

sources; later research also covered the eighteenth and nineteenth centuries, drawing materials from other sources as well. Thus, professionalization of Indian Christian history among Indian Catholics started long before Kaj Baago arrived in India. Perhaps professionalization among Orthodox, Marthoma, and Protestant students owes much to the inspiration and initiatives of Baago.

The general professionalization of Indian Christian history and the shift in perspective were on the increase from the 1960s onward. Kaj Baago's contribution to a radical shift is well described by Webster. Webster himself and many members of the reinvigorated Church History Association of India, like T. V. Philip and D. V. Singh, made important contributions toward this change in perspective. It is the cumulative result of these contributions that is expressed in the perspective drawn up by the Editorial Board of CHAI in 1973.

In the historiography analyzed, Webster noticed four important changes that had taken place from about 1824 to 1974. In the nineteenth century, the historians, publishers, and intended readers were all Western and mainly Protestant; in the twentieth century all of them had become Indians (St. Thomas Christians, as well as other Indian Christians of different denominations and rites). By the 1960s, both historians and readers were no longer exclusively Christian, but also Hindus and Muslims. With this change, the social and intellectual context broadened, and concerns of historians and their readers were not merely churchly preoccupations of the nineteenth century (Protestant versus Catholic, church and state, missionary methods, and so on), and also of the twentieth century (indigenization, unity and mission of the Indian church, and so on).

A second important change is the growing professionalization and the high expectation it placed on historians. The implication of this development is that from then on all Christian histories, whether scholarly or popular, must be based upon scholarly history. A third change is that Christian histories in India now are drawn from a far greater diversity of source materials than had been the case previously. This has necessitated a stricter discipline in approaching sources: the previous total confidence in the trustworthiness of the missionary records has been shaken, since conflicting evidence was found in Hindu, Muslim, or government sources.

Finally, the pace of change itself has changed. From Hough to Firth there is much continuity. Each historian relied heavily upon his predecessors for information, for methods, and for perspectives. Institutional continuity rather than break with the past is more impressive until we come to the 1960s, when there is a rapid diversification of the community of historians and readers, marked advances in the professionalization, and sharp change in perspectives introduced by advocates of indigenization and the academic historians. But many church historians have not been able to cope with this pace of change; perhaps even the CHAI history is not an exception, as at least portions of it may appear as a mixture of the new and the old.

CHAI History Perspective

From the foregoing analysis of Indian Christian historiography, it is clear why the Editorial Board of CHAI declared that the perspective from which the history of Christianity has been written in the past stood "in serious need of revision." The earlier histories, except what is reflected in some records about the historical consciousness of the ancient (St. Thomas) Christians of India or some histories written by them about themselves, treated the history of Christianity in India as an eastward extension of Western ecclesiastical history. Stress has been laid upon either its internal history or upon its "foreign mission" dimension so that the church is viewed as a relatively self-contained unit which acted upon and was acted upon by the society outside (CHAI, 1974: 89).

As Shenk notes, these histories swerved between two extremes: either an entirely internal and parochial viewpoint dominated or the "foreign mission" point of view. Both of these extremes reinforced the notion that Christianity was alien to Indian soil (1996: 54). In the past, many concerned Hindu thinkers (for example, K. C. Sen) have painfully pointed this out.

What was needed was a history that located the church firmly in the Indian historical context. It must describe Christian history as a real encounter of the Christian gospel with the soul of India, as the process of "the planting of the gospel inside" the Indian culture, the Indian philosophy, and the Indian religion (Baago, 1969: 85). Hence the CHAI Editorial Board proposed "to write the history of Christianity in the context of Indian history" by focusing attention upon the social-cultural history of the Christian people of India, by using a framework which is both ecumenical and national, and by using the region as their basic working unit. The four dimensions of an integral history of Christianity in India as defined in the perspective are social-cultural (the encounter dimension mentioned above), regional (a history that attends to the various diversities of India), national (the general reference being India as a whole), and ecumenical (looking at the Christianity of India as a whole). It is these last two dimensions that T. V. Philip has in mind when he says:

The history of the Indian Church...best understood as an independent story...is the common possession of all Christians of India. The history of Christianity in any part of India is an integral part of history of the Church anywhere in the country...much larger and richer than our denominational histories. (1972: 300)

If we were to apply to India the "center-periphery" paradigm proposed by EATWOT, especially Dussel, a picture like the following may be attempted. Perhaps until the sixteenth century, the East-Syrian (Persian) church acted as the "center" and the Indian church was the receiving end, the "periphery." In the sixteenth century, the colonial Padroado destroyed this central status of the East-Syrian church and imposed itself as the center. The Padroado first and the Propaganda later assumed this position. There was stout resistance against this attempt that paved the way for splits in the community. In the seventeenth century the West-Syrian Church of Antioch entered the scene and attempted to impose itself as the center vis-à-vis the Orthodox group of the St. Thomas Christians. In the eighteenth century, mission boards took the place of the center. Resistance started in the nineteenth century. The center status occupied by the Padroado and Propaganda from the sixteenth century onward, as far as the Catholics are concerned, is somehow reflected later in the Roman centralizing tendency. The Antioch-Indian tension continues to some extent in the Orthodox churches. As far as the Protestant and the Marthomite churches are concerned, perhaps administratively they are independent, except for some dependence for financial and educational help. Culturally, the hang-over of colonial and other dependencies continues as a burden of the past for all groups of Indian Christians.

The Task of Christian History Today and Tomorrow

The changing tasks that are set before Christian historians at the onset of the third millennium are to be derived from the world context and the Christian contexts that I have tried to delineate so far. Given the worldwide expansion of the church and the consequent altered identity, the changed world, and ecclesial reality, Christian historians should ask, What new approaches and what new perspectives are demanded of history? They will ask questions like the ones posed below and visualize the procedure to be adopted for their task. The answers will decide what sources are to be used, how they are to be interpreted, what methods are to be used, and what perspectives are to be adopted. The questions are as follows:

> Did the churches recognize the awakened national consciousness of peoples and their culture and religion after the decolonization process was complete? How have the alternatives to the sinister globalization worked in the churches? How are we to write the history of the new evangelization, the present cycle of evangelization in the "periphery"? How are we to proceed with a Christian history of, for, and by the poor?
>
> Has a new epoch emerged? If so, what are its implications for the churches? Have the churches taken serious note of these implications? Do they grasp the intercultural, multi-faceted, and integral dimensions of the present era? How do they react to them? Have the historians conceived of a new periodization of Christian history?
>
> What impact will the "new" history and the attempts to integrate it with the "old" have on Christian history? Will it help the search for a global Christian history? Has the early concept of independent local churches and of the church as a communion of churches reemerged in the second half of the twentieth century? How has that concept influenced Christian theology and history?

Having given these sample questions for writing Christian history in the future, I will now concentrate on the tasks of historians from a "Third Church," particularly from an Indian point of view.

Christian history in the third millennium must recognize the religious tradition of India, all religious traditions of the world for that matter, as part of God's universal plan of salvation. It must recognize that God has revealed himself to peoples of various religious traditions and ideologies, that they have experienced the Divine and its manifestations. The Christian historians of this century will carefully examine whether a really deep encounter of the heart of Christianity with the authentic and multifaceted soul of India (as well as the soul of Asia, Africa, Latin America, and the soul of the emerging new cultures of the rest of the world) has taken place. They will ask whether this encounter has changed the prevailing traditional form of Christianity and whether this encounter has changed the culture of India, of the rest of Asia, and of the world.

Christian history of the third millennium will examine how far a distinct Indian, an Asian, an African, or a Latin American Christian theology and praxis have come of age; how far they have been recognized all over the Christian world; how far these theologies and praxes have entered into mutual dialogue; how far their influence has been felt in other parts of the world, including the West; how far they have been able to help a growing realization that no particular theology or praxis or a particular institutional structure can be *the* theology or praxis or structure for the whole church at all times; how far these theologies and praxes have been able to shake the assumptions and foundations of traditional theologies and praxes of Western and Eastern Christendoms; and how far they have assumed the proportions of a challenge.

Christian history in the third millennium must recognize that not only the intellectual-philosophical resources but also the experiential and existential (the religious-cultural and sociopolitical) resources of different peoples are avenues for Christian encounter and Christian hermeneutics. Christian history in the third millennium must take seriously into consideration the attempts made by secular historians, anthropologists, and sociologists and acknowledge that these attempts enable Christian historians and Christian theologians to reread history and highlight neglected and forgotten events.

Indian Christian historians of the future are called upon to take a more critical and corrective approach in their utilization of the dominant Hindu religious resources, especially in the face of the traditional discrimination and social segregation of some one hundred and fifty million oppressed people (the *dalits*) of India. The authenticity of future Christian histories of India will depend upon how comprehensive (not selective) their approach is, since India is a mosaic of religions and cultures, a wide variety of languages, cultures, and ethnic groups that few countries in the world have.

The future Christian historians will explore how far the Christian church and her theology-praxis has come out of the closed circle of intellectuals and academicians and become truly the people's church, the people's theology, the people's worship, and the people's institutions. They will ask whether an Indian approach to theology has done away with a separation between orthodoxy and orthopraxis — and whether it has become a *sadhana* (an exercise) for the realization of the Divine; whether doing theology has ceased to be an exercise in borrowing and become an exercise springing from Indian roots in language and content, an exercise carried on by Indian thinkers and teachers who have their deep roots in the Indian religious-cultural context and not in Western or Eastern Christendom.

A historian of the third millennium will focus attention on how Christian thinkers and activists have been able to release the liberating force of the gospel, how they have been able to develop a theology and an action plan which addresses the situation of mass poverty, hunger, malnutrition, and illiteracy, which contributes to the transformation of a situation of the underprivileged and discriminated-against groups: the tribal people, the other oppressed groups, the women, the children. The future historian will ask how the people belonging to these groups are involved in a major way to take up leadership in the communities, as teachers, as pastors, as theologians, and as animators.

Indian historians will in the future examine how far the Christians have taken seriously the thoughts and lives of such Hindus, Buddhists, Sikhs, and Muslims, who are fascinated by the person and message of Jesus, who, rooted in their culture and tradition of the people and at the same time devoted and attached to Christ,[5] offer fresh insights into the Christian faith. They will examine whether a single Indian theology or praxis developed or a plurality of theologies and praxes developed, considering the composite and culturally multifaceted India and the existence of varied groups of Christians — Latin, Oriental, Catholic, Protestant, and Orthodox — and the existence of a variety of religious communities, theologies, and praxes stemming from distinctly regional and ecclesiastic varieties, from the experiences of distinct groups of people like the *dalits,* women, and so on. Two or three streams or strands of theology and praxis have developed in India: the spiritual-contemplative, the intellectual-philosophical, and the sociopolitical, or the *bhakti, jnana,* and *karma* strands. The future historian will examine how these different streams or strands have interacted and met, and whether a paradigm has emerged to provide a synthesis.

The Task for a Global Christian History

"Global" evokes mixed feelings today in the context of the use and misuse of the word "globalization" and the sinister connotations associated with it. The new Indian government, in the statement of its national agenda, admits the need for globalization, but it has to be a "calibrated" globalization. The government feels that it should have the sovereign inalienable right to choose its economic system as well as its legal, social, cultural, and political system in accordance with its historic traditions, national genius, and the express will of its people (*The Hindu,* 1998: 14). Wilbert R. Shenk in his article, "Towards a Global Christian History," keeps a balanced view of the global, as he stresses equality and parity. I have read with interest his findings, made through a survey of a

---

5. K. C. Sen, P. C. Mozoomdar, Vivekananda, Mahatma Gandhi, Subba Rao, and so on.

series of related literature, and his constructive suggestions. He is quite right when he says that the writing of non-Western church history does not by itself fulfill the vision of global church history. The encouraging developments over the last fifty years are an important contribution, but only a partial corrective. Our task is to conceptualize and produce a truly global church history. This attempt must overcome long-standing obstacles and the burden of the past: the undertow of tradition, the general neglect of the majority church in Western historiography, and the bias against mission. Shenk proposes the development of an approach of parity, an intercultural approach to history to realize the goal of a global church history. He also provides a model for the same, based on the insights of Paul A. Cohen, who investigated how the history of China has been written over the past 150 years.

As already observed, the perspective of CHAI history proposes national and ecumenical dimensions as the general point of reference. At the same time, it gives equal importance to the regional and denominational aspects. It is an approach of parity: avoiding privileging any one group and giving maximum attention to regional expressions of the faith. All together form the national or ecumenical (intercultural) history of Indian Christians. I am tempted to recall here St. Paul's comparison of the church with the human body (1 Cor. 12): all members of the body are of equal importance and each has its specific function without which the body will not remain in its integrity. Integrity demands that parts are accepted on their own terms. I have written a book, *Indian Christians: Search for Identity and Struggle for Autonomy* (1984), in which I identify the elements of the selfhood of each unit of the Indian church. The last chapter is "Quest for an Indian Church." It emphasizes the relationship of "parity, reciprocity, and mutual dependence," suggested by Shenk as elements of global church history.

Giving importance to the regional and denominational, even to the Indian identity should not mean "parochializing." In India, perhaps in all the previously colonial countries, anti-colonialism and anti-Western sentiments, when exaggerated, turn out to be a sort of parochialism. The recent reactions in certain circles in India against some program conceived in connection with the anniversary of Vasco da Gama's arrival in India smacks of such parochialism (the attitude of "we have nothing to do with Gama; we have nothing to do with the West"). So too the *dalit* (the oppressed classes)-oriented histories, "history from below," sometimes tend to be prejudicial against the high-caste culture. (Even the mention of "brahman-sanskritic" culture is anathema to some *dalit* enthusiasts.) Such histories can be hijacked, as Romila Thapar says, for purposes of regional (or national) chauvinism. Otherwise, these historians have a message, the message contained in the cluster of insights provided by the studies of Leenhardt ("acculturation in two directions") and Fairbank ("cultural stimulus and responsibility in both directions"), and the special meaning "translation" gets in the particular context of mission. These insights are of prime importance in our movement toward a global church history which, according to Shenk, must have the following marks: recognition that "our history" is not only our regional or national history, but part of the world church history; recognition that the local is essential, because there can be no global apart from the local; recognition of the power of narrative and social history; and, finally, recognition of the meaning of the church as "its capacity to incarnate the life of God revealed in Jesus Christ among all peoples, in all places, and in all times." The People of God can no longer afford to live in the era of the "Western" or "Eastern" or any other parochialism. A global church history must celebrate cultural authenticity combined with ecclesial unity (1996: 56).

The remarks Hans Küng (1964) made about an ecumenical council may well be borne in mind by historians attempting a global Christian history. All the individual churches so different from one another; scattered throughout the *oikumene* in all countries and continents; made up of all races, languages, and cultures; belonging to societies with different political social structures; and having different rites, liturgies, theologies, and forms of piety and laws, by virtue of their assemblage constitute and realize the visible-invisible unity of the whole church. It is a concrete actualization of the unity of the different, heterogeneous, independent churches with their own problems and difficulties, needs, concerns, and demands. That is unity, catholicity in pluralism.

In the emerging picture of historiography in general, as referred to earlier, the new and the traditional seem to be gradually converging. The new epoch is marked by convergence rather than divergence. In general, in Indian historiography, regional or local histories, if not hijacked for purposes of regional chauvinism, can usefully act as a correction to easy generalization. These insights are of great importance when we consider a global Christian history.

As the new and traditional are to be seen as complementary and not contradictory, so the church as a whole and these different local churches are complementary and not contradictory. Neither can exist alone. The whole church is present in the particular church, since Christ and his Spirit are really present in it. The universal church is a reality only by virtue of the particular churches, and these are true churches only through being in communion with one another (Bühlman, 1977: 272). This is the foundation for a global Christian history. According to Archbishop Quinn, the fundamental concern of the ecclesial mode (as different from the political mode) is communion and discernment in faith of the diversity of the gifts and works of the Spirit. The claims of discernment and the claims of order (which may be interpreted as control to ensure unity) must always coexist, for one cannot be embraced and the other rejected (Quinn, 1997: 66).

EATWOT members speak of a genuine globalization as referred to earlier. It is against this globalization perspective that a global Christian history is to be conceived. The specificity of local churches must be taken seriously, and history should be written in such a way as to be for the development of the awareness of these churches today. From these regional positions, a new world vision of the church and its history, a global analogy, may perhaps emerge; in other words, a vision constructed from the differences and specificities of each in the light of the similarity deriving from our common Christianity (Dussel, 1985: 12). All communion involves an exchange of experiences, the placing at the common disposal of all what affects the community, the common quest of the common good. There can be communion only when the members of a community regard one another as equals, as brothers and sisters, each person with their function. Any church community must exist for service to others and not power (Boff, 1991: 89).

In conclusion, I make reference to the nineteenth-century Hindu genius, Keshub Chunder Sen (1838–84), not because Sen was interested in a global Christian history, but because he entertained a global vision which is inspiring for the concept of a global Christian history. Sen was one of those nineteenth-century Indian Renaissance young intellectuals who had received a good English education and been deeply influenced by a Western secular and religious outlook; who looked to Western enlightenment and Christian religion as sources for reforming and renewing Hindu society from within; who longed for a healthy marriage between the East and the West; and who looked forward to an era in which a genuine Indian heritage would shine forth with added luster when illuminated by the fresh light from the West. In attempts to interpret Christianity as a fulfillment of Hinduism as well as in attempts to "Orientalize" Christ and Christianity, this quest for the marriage between the East and West is strongly evident. K. C. Sen who was a "Christian," short of baptism and membership in any Christian denomination, was perhaps the first Indian to perceive clearly the positive implications of bringing about a harmony between the Indian religious values and the spiritual content of the religion of Christ (Mundadan, 1997: 312–35).

By the late 1860s, Sen appears as an admirer of the "enlightened nations of the West" and praises Providence for relating India to it through "the hands of a Christian sovereign" (the queen of England). Sen appreciates the various advantages of the British and European connection. He sees in this connection an opportunity provided by Divine Providence for effecting a harmony between the West and the East.[6] He derives great satisfaction from his discovery that Christ and the apostles who propagated the gospel were Asiatics. That thought adds to his patriotic feelings as an Asian.

Sen began to conceive the idea of his *Navavidhan* ("The Church of the New Dispensation" which, according to him, is the "The Future Church") at least from 1869 onward. Even before, he was moving toward the idea (his lectures, "Jesus Christ: Europe and Asia" and "Great Men," both delivered in 1866, initiate the idea). In 1869, in his lecture on "The Future Church," he defined the future church as both indigenous and universal. The future religion of the world will be the common religion of all nations, but in each nation it will have an indigenous growth; from the depths of the life of each nation its future church will naturally grow up.

After his visit to England (1869), Sen became all the more convinced that England had much to learn from India, as India from England (think of Leenhardt's "acculturation in two directions" or Fairbank's "cultural stimulus and responsibility in both directions," or "translation" dependent on both the natives and the missionaries), the West from the East, and the East from the West. England must accept from India "the very spirit of devotion and prayer which Jesus Christ tried to inculcate. . . . Let India . . . learn from England practical righteousness. Let England learn from India faith and prayer" (Scott, 1979).

Navavidhan was launched in 1879. It was the Christ-centered (not Christianity-centered) harmony of all scriptures and prophets and dispensations, "the sweet music of divine instruments," "the celestial court where, around enthroned divinity shine the light of all heavenly saints and prophets." It had united the East and the West, Asiatic and European faiths and characters. He concludes his 1883 lecture on "Asia's Message to Europe" with his image of the final consummation of the Church of the New Dispensation:

---

6. Sen belonged to that group of nineteenth-century thinkers who took a "providential" view of British rule in India. But that view has been totally rejected by mainstream nationalist thinkers.

And as the new song of Atonement is sung with enthusiasm by a million voices, representing all the various languages of the world, a million souls, each dressed in its national garb of piety and righteousness, glowing in an infinite and complete variety of colors, shall dance round and round the Father's throne and peace and joy shall reign forever. (Scott, 1979: 289)

This passage reminds me of the task set for global church history, "to celebrate cultural authenticity combined with ecclesial unity."

THREE

MISSION HISTORY VERSUS CHURCH HISTORY

The Case of China Historiography

Philip Yuen-Sang Leung

Writing history is a quest for truth and reality, but it is also a personal search for self-identity.

Historiographic traditions represent various forms of collective memories; yet they are also expressions of different cultural mentalities.

Writing Mission History and Writing Chinese Church History: Some Personal Reflections

It is my intention to reevaluate the notions of "mission history," "church history," and "Christian history" in light of the paradigmatic shifts and methodological changes in the historical discipline and the coming of age of Christianity as a truly global religion, and to redefine the relationship of mission history and church history through a reexamination of the history and historiography of the Christian missions and church communities in China. Before I begin reviewing the historiographic traditions in regard to the missionary movement in China and the history of the Chinese church, I would like to indulge in some self-reflections on my own experience in writing mission history and Chinese church history. For me, teaching and writing history is a professional career, but researching and writing the history of the Christian church in China means much more to me than a professional business; it is also part and parcel of my soul searching and emotional identification, which began almost thirty years ago.

My first book, *Young J. Allen in China: His Careers and the Wanguo Gongbao,* published twenty years ago in Hong Kong (1978), is about the life and work of an American missionary in China from 1860 to 1907. It originated from my postgraduate research from 1972 to 1974 at the Chinese University of Hong Kong. At that time, I was a young Chinese scholar who had committed his life to Christ. Motivated by a sense of duty as a Christian historian and as a concerned member of the Chinese church engaged in a passionate search for self-identity, I was deeply interested in finding out more about the history of the Christian church in China. I was looking for ways to bridge the gap between the spheres of academic scholarship and the needs of emotional identification. The historical research, in fact, became simultaneously a search for intellectual commitment and self-identity for me as a Chinese Christian intellectual. When I embarked on that journey of search and research in the early 1970s, I followed the path laid down half a century ago by a predecessor in the 1920s. In my effort to uncover the history of Christianity in China, I had chosen the "mission history" approach of the eminent historian Professor Kenneth S. Latourette of Yale University; his monumental work, *A History of the Christian Missions in China,* first published in 1929 and reprinted several times in later decades, would become my principal reference and important guidebook. As I began my graduate project in 1972, I chose an American missionary as the focus of my research with the hope that through the project I would learn more about the Christian church in China in addition to obtaining my academic credentials. Academically, my advisors praised my dissertation on the life and work of Young J. Allen, the American missionary from the Methodist Episcopal Mission, South, who came to China in 1860 and died in China in 1907, and it won a publishing grant from the Harvard-Yenching Institute. The resultant book, published by the Chinese University of Hong Kong Press in 1978, has been described by Hong Kong historians as one of the pioneer studies in Chinese church history (see Wong and Lee, 1994; Lee, 1998); I believe this is a mislabel, since the book is a study of missionary history, a genre well established and used by Western scholars within the field of mission history or mission studies. But the book was quite well received by the Chinese academic community on both sides of the Straits. In Mainland China it played a small part in stirring up intellectual interest in the history of Christianity in China, particularly among a group of young scholars who grew up under the anti-foreign and anti-Christian teachings of Maoist Communism and now turned to Western culture in the initial phase of Deng Xiaoping's Reform Era.

When I started out to write a history on the American missionary Young J. Allen and his Methodist Episcopal Mission, South, I was not aware of the differences between "mission history" and "church history." My research on Allen did increase my knowledge, as it was intended, about the Chinese church in the nineteenth century, particularly the history of the Episcopalians and Methodists in Shanghai and East China. At the same time, it also expanded my intellectual horizons into the outer world beyond the Chinese church, beyond China, and beyond my original expectations — to knowledge of American Protestantism, the missionary movement in Victorian England and postbellum America, and the organization and financing of the home missions. At the end of that research process, my original goals of searching for self-identity and for a better understanding of the Chinese church through such an intellectual endeavor were only partially fulfilled as my work was mission-based and missionary-centered. As a result, I had learned more about American missions than about the Chinese church. In retrospect, I would describe my first book as a product of mission history — rather than Chinese church history — from which the faces and feelings of foreign missionaries have come through much better than that of the Chinese Christians, most of whom would remain nameless, faceless, and unclear if not totally unknown, even in their own land, in their own community, and in the treatment by their own historians.

To me, a better understanding of the differences between mission history and Chinese church history came in the late 1970s as a result of the shift in academic trends in writing the history of modern China. As superbly summarized and described by Professor Paul A. Cohen in his book *Discovering History in China* (1984), the China historians in America began to move away from the Western-centric perspectives of the post–World War II decades from the 1940s to the 1970s to a China-centered consciousness in historical research and writing (ibid.: 149–98).

Since the early 1980s I have been devoting my time and energy to emphasizing the "other." As I began my quest from the mission or missionary view, the "other" actually became "ourselves." In studying and researching the history of Christianity in China, the focus should, I argued emphatically, be on the receiving end of the missionary enterprise — the Chinese end, that is, the Chinese Christians. I began to campaign enthusiastically, first in Singapore and then in Hong Kong and America, for a shift of research focus from the history of missions and missionaries to the history of the Chinese Christian communities and local and indigenous Christian institutions. I began to collect biographical data of Chinese church pastors and conversion experiences of Chinese Christians, primarily from a familiar source — the *Jiaohui Xinbao* [*Church News*] — an early Chinese journal published in the nineteenth century and edited, ironically, by Allen the missionary.[1] While I was thinking and working in this direction in the 1980s, I was especially pleased to see the publication of two books in the field, one in Chinese, *Zhongguo Jidujiao renwu xiaochuan* (1983) by Professor Cha Shih-chieh of the National Taiwan University, and one in English, *Chinese Christians: Elites, Middlemen, and the Church in Hong Kong* by Carl Smith (1985), a missionary-turned-historian. Both scholars shared my concern. The Reverend Carl Smith raised the following question in the preface of his book: "[In writing the history of the Chinese church], this emphasis on the missionary troubled me.... Should not the emphasis be on the Chinese end of the story" (ibid.: xiii)?

Why, in the history of Christian missions in China, were there only a few Chinese working for God, and others were all "faceless"? I have taken what I called "Carl's Challenge" to my Christian friends in Hong Kong, Taiwan, and China and pushed my research students to work in this direction. My own research, as a result of this new realization, has been on a mission — *to rediscover the Chinese in Chinese church history.* My research since has been focusing on the Chinese end of the missions story, on Chinese Christian leaders, and on the Chinese Christian communities (in Lee, 1987: 66–89). Under my encouragement and guidance my students have done research on Wang Yuanshen and his sons (Bingyao and Xuchu), Liu Tingfang, Jing Dianying, Liu Liangmo, Wang Jixin, Wei Zuomin, Zhao Zichen, Wu Yaozhong, and others. These were either Chinese Christian leaders or pastors and theologians. Xing Fuzang (Hsing Fu-tsang) (1997) has broken new ground by working on Christian lay leaders who were prominent leaders of the military and of the government during the Republican period. His doctoral dissertation on Xu Qian, Feng Yuxiang, and Zhang Zhijiang, completed in 1994 at the Chinese University of Hong Kong, came out in book form in 1997. Professor Peter Ng Tze Ming, my colleague in the Department of Religion at the Chinese University of Hong Kong, has been working on mission schools and Christian colleges for quite some time and has found a new research focus on the Chinese leaders in higher education (see Ng, 1996: 106–8). My friend at the Hong Kong Baptist University,

---

1. I remember the idea and plan of collecting biographical data on Chinese pastors and lay leaders and their writings from the *Jiaohui Xinbao* [*Chiao-hui hsin-pao* or *Church News*] was first presented to Professor Daniel Bays to be considered as a part of the "Christianity in China Project" in 1984–85. Later I was pleased that the Bays project had put much effort into investigating the interactions between missions and Chinese society. See Daniel Bays, ed., *Christianity in China: From the Eighteenth Century to the Present* (Stanford: Stanford University Press, 1996).

Professor Lee Kam-keung, who teaches a course of the history of Christianity in China, also shares this vision. He is instrumental in building the archive on the history of Christianity in China at Baptist University and launching an academic journal for the study of Christianity in China. He himself has published articles on Huang Naishang and Hu Liyuan, the former a Methodist leader in Fujian and the latter a Hong Kong Christian in the late Qing dynasty (Lee, 1997a: 189–212; and 1997b: 53–71). Kwok Pui-lan has carried on this campaign and pushed it further by focusing on Chinese Christian women. She says,

> When scholars chose to study Chinese Christians, they tended to focus on the lives and thought of male Christians and their responses to social change at the time. Even when female Christians were mentioned, they were invariably referred to as passive recipients of Christian benevolence, downtrodden objects to be emancipated, or feeble souls to be instructed and uplifted. Until fairly recently, Christian women were studied as missiological objects rather than historical subjects in the encounter between China and Christianity. (1996: 194)

This same statement could be applied to the study of the history of all Chinese Christians, male and female, two decades ago. The Chinese church then was at the margins of mission history. After two decades of development in historical research beginning in the 1970s, the margins have gradually become the mainstream. In my opinion, the shift of focus from mission history to the history of Chinese Christians in recent years has produced some visible results.

The study of the history of Christianity, particularly the expansion and growth of it as a world religion, however, inevitably involves the investigation of activities and ideas at both ends — the giving and the receiving. In the case of China historiography, the emphasis in the past decades was on the missionary end but in recent years has shifted toward the Chinese end. My own work over the last two decades epitomizes this shift of focus. Some American China historians are also moving in the same direction (such as Jessie G. Lutz), but, as I shall argue in the last section, the dichotomization and polarization of mission history versus Chinese church history is not necessarily the best way to deal with mission history or Chinese church history. The culture-conscious and race-conscious approaches, whether they are China-centered or mission-centered or Western-centered, only tend to divide the academic and the Christian communities, and not unite them. I shall argue that interrelatedness, interaction, inclusion, and intersections are better conceptual points and methods to be considered in our rethinking and reconstructing of the history of Christianity in China.

Before I return to the discussion of this paradigm shift and the alternatives, let me first discuss some of the issues related to the mission history approach.

Mission History in Western Perspective

"Mission history" is the history of the expansion of Christianity into non-Christian lands and is mission-based and missionary-centered. In the following, I shall discuss how this approach from two different points of view — one from a religious perspective and the other a secular perspective — formed the dominating framework in Western mission historiography in the past decades. First, let us look at mission history from a Christian perspective.

Labor of Love: Servants of God and Helpers of Man

From the Christian viewpoint we understand the need for world salvation and the expansion of the kingdom of God. We also understand that the most important force behind the missionary movement was religious, that is, the Christian obligation and commitment to the Great Commission of Jesus Christ, and not political or economic motivations. On the other hand, we also realize that the single-mindedness of the religious devotees and the mere support of the church were not the only fabrics of the missionary movement. Missions and missionaries were not operating from the heaven above but situated in a socio-politico-cultural context. Their work and their values were inseparably linked to the society and country they grew up in and the government and political system under which their missions were operated. The divine and the mundane, the sacred and the secular, could not be easily separated or clearly distinguished. When we identify with the religious goals of the missions and understand the Christian commitment to evangelism, we are mostly inclined to view mission history from the positive. From this vantage point, missionaries were seen as servants of God and helpers of their fellow humans. And this perspective has been translated into a tradition in mission historiography, an "exalted tradition," as I prefer to call it. Most missionary biographies and histories of missions published by Christian publishers belong to this category. They are not "histories" in the strict modern academic sense but historical literature for exaltation and Christian education purposes. In the case of China, examples of mission history in this mode are aplenty; the several biographies of James Hudson Taylor, the founder of the China Inland Mission, are exemplars of mission history of this mode. The earliest Taylor biography, also the most detailed version, was written by the missionary's own son, who himself was a missionary. He might know much more about his father and the China Inland Mission (CIM) than anyone else, especially the intimate things in the family and the inner feelings and emotions of Taylor. However, his intimacy and his own involvement in the enterprise might also become his limitation as a historian. Another Taylor biography, *Hudson Taylor and China's Open Century* in seven volumes and written by A. J. Broomhall (1981–89), an ex-missionary of CIM himself, also portrays Taylor as a pathfinder and pioneer evangelist who overcame all odds to bring the gospel to the Chinese. Another volume by William Speer, published in 1990 by the Overseas Missionary Fellowship, which is an extension of the China Inland Mission, also shares the same view. There were many more missionary biographies of this kind. Two that come to mind are the biographies of two pioneer missionaries to China: *Memoirs of the Life and Labors of Robert Morrison* (1839) and *The Life and Labors of Elijah Coleman Bridgman* (1866); both works were written by the missionaries' wives. There are many more biographies: Young J. Allen, Timothy Richard, Jonathan Goforth, Griffith John, Laura Haygood, and L. Nelson Bell (Mrs. Billy Graham's father), to name only a few. They were written either from the Christian education perspective, aiming at bolstering the Christian spirit, or from the denominational viewpoint, aiming at arousing passion and support for mission. In other words, a great many of these missionary biographies are more hagiographic than historical. This is not to say that they are not accurate in historical facts, but the interpretations are intended to support mission and the presentation is usually filled with emotions and exaltations. In this historiographic tradition, missionaries have been portrayed mostly as heroes or martyrs, rarely as full human beings with frailties and faults.

Another category in the Christian historiographic tradition is "denominational history." Protestant Christianity was and is organized into denominations such as Presbyterian, Methodist, Anglican, Congregationalist, Baptist, and others. Many denominations established their mission boards and sent out missionaries to China and other parts of the world. Denominational history is history of the work of missions and missionaries centering on one or more denominations. Some examples are Edward Band's *Working His Purpose Out: The History of the English Presbyterian Mission, 1847–1947*, published by the Presbyterian Church of England (London, 1948), and Richard Lovett's two-volume *The History of the London Missionary Society*, published in 1899. Norman Goodall extended this history with a volume in 1954. Another major British mission that was active in China, the Church Missionary Society (CMS), commissioned Eugene Stock to write its centennial history, entitled *The History of the Church Missionary Society: Its Environment, Its Men, and Its Work* (CMS, 1899, 3 vols.), followed by a two-volume history by Gordon Hewitt in 1977. Representing the Baptist denomination is *The History of the Baptist Missionary Society, 1792–1992* by Brian Stanley. As for the China missions, there are denominational histories written by "official" or "commissioned" historians such as Richard T. Baker's *Ten Thousand Years: The Story of Methodism's First Century in China* (1947) and Warren Candler's *Young J. Allen: The Man Who Seeded China* (1931), representing viewpoints of their respective denominations. Another form of denominational history concerns the organization and structure of history writing. In either mission history or Chinese church history, the denominational divisions are used as a convenient format in which the history of missions (personnel as well as activities) is organized. The famous volume of Donald MacGillivray's *A Century of Protestant Missions in China* (1907) and also M. T. Stauffer's *The Christian Occupation of China* (1922) and Latourette's *A History of Christian Missions in China* (1929) are not strictly denominational, but materials are organized primarily according to denominational lines. As we shall see in the following section, Chinese Christians also followed this model in writing the history of their own past in modern China.

In other words, in the Christian historiographic tradition — as far as the China field is concerned — missionary heroes, martyrs, the mainline denominations, and the home missions based in Europe and America dominate the shaping forces of history. The history writing process has not taken seriously the role of the Chinese converts and the domestic sociocultural forces in China.

Agents of Change: Catalyst of Social Reform and Modernization

In the field of mission studies in the West, especially in America, a growing number of publications in recent decades have come from secular academic institutions such as Harvard University. "Missions studies" or "missionary studies," in fact, have been part of America's "area studies," which emerged after World War II out of political concerns and Cold War mentality. In an effort to understand the history and culture of the developing countries or potential "enemies" of the post–World War II era, America's academia encouraged the study of Southeast Asia (particularly Vietnam), Latin America, and East Asia. China studies has been an important field within this new politico-academic framework. Under the influence of John K. Fairbank, research on modern Chinese history in the 1950s and 1960s had two important focuses:

how China responded to the challenges of the West, and how China's modernization (Westernization) movement began. Both themes involved the work of the Christian missions and the influence of missionaries. But the secular studies of the 1950s and 1960s do not usually present a positive view of the missionary. Oftentimes, the secular academics were rather critical in their evaluation of the missions. For example, Arthur Schlesinger Jr., writing in the early 1970s, maintained that "American missions ... represented the purposeful aggression of American culture against the ideas and cultures of other people" (1974: 336–73). Secular historians were more interested in probing the complex psychology of these missionaries and in pointing out their problems as well as analyzing their failures rather than promoting religion. They do not follow the Christian paradigm of mission history, but these studies are nevertheless centered on the missions and missionaries.

Despite criticisms of mission work, one positive theme in these academic studies of missions and missionaries stands out; that is, the Christian missions in general and some of the liberal missionaries in particular were agents of change in modern China. Their social involvement and cultural activities had a profound impact on a generation of reform-minded Chinese intellectuals in the late nineteenth and early twentieth centuries, who contributed significantly to reform and modernization in China. These Chinese reformers and modernizers, through their connections and acquaintance with the Christian missionaries, learned more about the outside world, and in turn helped stimulate change and reform in their own society. These Chinese intellectuals were not necessarily Christians themselves, and they did not accept everything the missionary told them. However, to them the missionary was a source of Western knowledge and an inspiration for reform and modernization. The following are some exemplary works: James C. Thomson's *While China Faced West: American Reformers in Nationalist China, 1928–1937* (Harvard, 1969) stressed the role of missionaries in Nationalist reforms; Irwin T. Hyatt Jr.'s *Our Ordered Lives Confess: Three Nineteenth-Century American Missionaries in Eastern Shantung* (Harvard, 1976) emphasized the role of missionaries in modern China's educational change and social reform; Jessie G. Lutz's *China and the Christian Colleges* (Cornell, 1971) focused on Christian missions' contribution to China's higher education; and Paul Richard Bohr's *Famine in China and the Missionary* (Harvard, 1972) looked at missionaries' role in charities and philanthropic activities in late nineteenth-century China.[2]

---

2. A detailed list of Western monographs analyzing the relations between missionaries and

Mission History from Chinese Perspectives

We have examined, although very briefly, the basic viewpoints in mission histori-ography regarding China in the English-speaking world. Now let us turn to the Chinese historical writings on foreign missions and missionaries. We can again divide the literature in the field into the two main categories used in the previous section: those from Christian viewpoints and those from non-Christian perspectives. The latter comes first.

Cultural Imperialism: Church Working for State

The viewpoint that dominated Chinese scholarship on Christian missions in the People's Republic of China (PRC) before the Reform Era amounts to a complete denunciation of the Christian contribution to China's modern trans-formation. For several decades, Chinese scholars had been analyzing the history of Christian missions from the "imperialism" framework. All Western powers were labeled by the Marxist scholars in the PRC as "imperialists," who came to exploit China's resources and establish a Western hegemony in Asia. Three important groups — diplomats, merchants, and missionaries — worked hand-in-hand in realizing their imperialist goals in China. (Li Shiyue, Hu Sheng, and Gu Changsheng are the leading historians in the PRC in this area of study, and they all shared this perspective.) Missionaries, in other words, were seen as one main component of imperialism and colonialism; that is, an integral part of the Western intrusion into China. They were assisting their governments in a variety of ways: gathering intelligence for trade, economic development, and military purposes; recruiting agents and collaborators; changing minds by spreading and promoting Western values and by serving as interpreters for diplomats; and, not rarely, by becoming political representatives themselves. In other words, the Chinese scholars see an intimate church-state relationship in expanding Western imperialism. In their eyes, there was very little altruism in missionary endeavor. Before the 1980s, the leading scholar whose research covered the activities of foreign missionaries in China was Li Shiyue. Li sees the missionaries as the main source of conflict involving disputes between local Chinese communities and foreigners in all "jiao-an" (anti-Christian) cases. He denounces the missionaries as intruders and imperialists who used religion to

China's modernization can be found in note 14 of Robert (1994: 159). The latest state-of-the-field article is by Lutz (1998: 31–54).

"enslave the Chinese" and advance the economic and political goals of their governments (see Li, 1962).[3]

It is no surprise that there was only one dominating viewpoint in PRC in the period from 1949 to 1979 because of the emphasis on political ideology and the strong grip of the Communist Party on academics. But when we turn to the historical writings by the anti-Communist Chinese scholars in Taiwan, we are amazed that many of them share the anti-Christian and anti-missionary sentiment of their counterparts in Communist China. The first generation of modern China specialists at the Institute of Modern History of the Academia Sinica at Nangang, Taipei, produced a voluminous set of archival materials on missions affairs and missionary cases (see Lu Shih-chiang, 1959–81). Like the Communist Chinese historians, they saw missionary evangelism as a source of Sino-Western disputes. The tone was not as political as the jargon-filled politicized literature in the PRC, but the perspective on Christian missions as helpers of foreign governments and a source of Sino-Western conflict was very much the same (see Lu, 1966; Lee, 1998: 10–11). In fact, this anti-Christian attitude of Chinese intellectuals shared by the Left and the Right despite their own political differences seemed to be deeply rooted in the intellectual tradition of modern China. This anti-Christian stance could perhaps be traced back to the "Anti-Christian Movement" of the May Fourth era in the 1920s during which Christianity was attacked by both Chen Duxiu and Hu Shi (see Lutz, 1988; Yip, 1980; and Yeh, 1992). However, in Taiwan we soon see a changing attitude toward mission history in the academy. Increasingly, diverse opinions in interpreting mission history appeared in the 1960s and 1970s as the field of modern Chinese studies became more internationalized (or, more specifically, Americanized) as demonstrated by the popularity of the modernization theory and other Western-imported methodologies in historical interpretation. Influenced by Western scholarship, the Chinese historians in Taiwan were more inclined to see missionaries as agents of reform and modernization although the imperialism interpretation still prevailed as an important framework.

Returning to the state of the field in the Mainland, since the early 1980s there has been a growing interest among Chinese scholars in the history of Christianity in general and in the research of missionary history. According to a survey, there were more than 500 articles published in scholarly journals in this area in only a decade, outnumbering all scholarly output in the first thirty years of PRC history (Ho, 1994: 125). The major works published in the 1980s

---

3. For a summary of Li's views, see Tao, 1998: 56–57.

include Gu Changsheng's two books, *Chuanjiaoshi yu jindai Zhongguo* [Foreign Missionaries in Modern China] (Shanghai, 1981) and *Cong Malixu dao Situ Leideng* [From Robert Morrison to John Leighton Stuart] (Shanghai, 1985); Jiang Wenhan's *Zhongguo gudai di Jidujiao yu Kaifeng di Youtairen* [A History of Christianity in Ancient China and the Jews in Kaifeng] (Beijing, 1982) and *Ming-Qing jian cai Hua di Tianzhujiao Yesu huishi* [The Catholic Jesuits in China during the Ming-Qing Period] (Beijing, 1989); Zhang Li and Liu Jiantang, *Zhongguo Jiaoan shi* [A History of "Missionary Cases" in China] (Chengdu, 1987); and Li Chucai, editor, *Diguo zhuyi chinhua jiaoyushi ziliao* [A Documentary History of Imperialist Encroachment in China's Education] (Beijing, 1987). It is not an exaggeration to say that "missionary research" has emerged as a sub-field of historical studies in the PRC, but the Chinese scholars of the 1980s did not seem quite liberated yet from their past influences. Essentially, their views deviated little from the official partisan perspective of the past. Foreign missionaries are portrayed in these recent publications as collaborators with imperialism. For example, Gu Changsheng's two volumes, though well-organized and smoothly written, with bountiful archival materials and rich historical data, conveyed nevertheless the same message: missions as cultural imperialism. Their work in planting churches, establishing schools and hospitals, organizing relief and charitable activities, and promoting social and political reforms was all a part of the plan to Christianize and Westernize China, and aimed at perpetuating Western dominance in the world. In their writings, the Chinese scholars might have toned down a bit the anti-imperialist outcry or dropped the Marxist anti-imperialist jargon altogether, but the underlying theme of these books and articles was still that of "cultural imperialism."

The real breakthrough in Chinese scholarship in the field of missions studies and missionary history came only in the past few years with the emergence of a generation of young scholars and junior professors. They have traveled outside China, visiting missionary archives and Christian universities in the West, and have adopted a variety of approaches to the study of history of Christianity in China. Many of them have shown sympathy to and understanding of the problems faced by foreign missionaries in China, and they also acknowledge the religious devotion and efforts by the missionaries in social reform and philanthropic activities.[4] Some examples are Shi Jinghuan's *Dikaowen he Situ Leideng caihua dijiaoyu huodong* [The Educational Activities of Calvin Mateer and John

---

4. The young scholars I know include Xu Yihua, Shi Jinghuan, and Tao Feiya, to name a few. Xu, whose research covers Christian higher education and Shanghai missions, obtained his Ph.D. from Princeton University; Shi had traveled extensively in America before and after

Leighton Stuart in China] (Taipei, 1991), Tao Feiya, *Chuanjiaoshi yu Shandong jindai shehui* [Missionaries and Social Transformation in Modern Shandong] (Beijing, 1994), and Wang Lixin, *Meiguo chuanjiaoshi yu wanqing Zhongguo xiandaihua* [American Missionaries and Modernization of China in the Late Qing Dynasty] (Tianjin, 1997). Wang Lixin, for example, asserts that the Christian missionaries who came to China in the nineteenth and twentieth centuries were unlike the political representatives and business adventurers, and their primary reason for coming to China was for religious and evangelistic work. He also thinks that the missionaries played a positive role in the introduction of Western science and culture to the Chinese. However, in the end, Wang also criticized the missionaries "for shaping China's modernization according to the goals and interests of the Christian church and the Western world," but "history has shown that the modernization of China was unlikely to follow the pattern designed by missionaries and will be realized only after the efforts of generations of progressive Chinese on the basis of independent choice and with the initiative in their own hands" (Wang, 1997: 2).

The Brother's Keeper: Where Was the Little Brother?

After a brief review of the non-Christian views of the Chinese on mission history, let us now turn to the Christian minorities. How did the Chinese Christians in the earlier decades view the history of foreign missions in China? And how did they evaluate the history of their own church in modern history? It is not an overstatement to say that the majority of the Chinese Christians in the past had generally ignored the history of Christianity in their own country, and there was little organized effort in promoting or supporting serious investigations of Chinese church history by Christian scholars. Wang Zhixin's *Zhongguo Jidujiao, shigang* [A Brief History of Christianity in China], published in the 1940s, had been used by seminaries for a long time as the only textbook for Chinese church history. Two other histories on the same subject, written and printed earlier in the 1920s or 1930s by Xie Honglai and Chen Jinyong, had been lost without a trace (Wang, 1997: 16). Many Chinese Christian leaders liked to emphasize spiritual renewal and rebirth, hence implying and encouraging a departure from rather than a continued association with their own cultural past. Writings from Liang Zhuchen and Lin Xianzhen in the *Church News* [*Jiaohui Xinbao*] and the sermons of Wang Mingdao and Song Shangjie

---

writing her book on Mateer and Stuart; and Tao spent some time in Santa Barbara and Hong Kong for research on missionaries and Christian higher education in Shandong.

all attested to an evangelical and spiritual emphasis within the Chinese church tradition. I suspect the same emphasis could be found in other Asian churches such as those in Korea. For example, a testimony of a famous Korean Christian leader, Yun Chi-ho (1867–1945), reads:

> I had not heard of God before I came to Shanghai,
> for I was born in a heathen land,
> I was brought up in a heathen society,
> I was taught in heathen literature.
>
> (Quoted in Paik, 1980: 166)

The emphasis was on discontinuity and disassociation with the "heathen" history and culture. As a result of this negligence or denial of its own history and tradition (a phenomenon that was so markedly different from traditional Confucian culture, which valued historical consciousness and cultural continuities, and is, I think, an important issue that deserves separate attention), the Chinese church had relied more on mission histories by Westerners, such as Latourette's, to rediscover and relearn their own past. Most of the Chinese church members in Hong Kong and Taiwan had easy access to the hagiographic literature on missionary heroes and martyrs from the West through Chinese translations. From these sources, they began the endeavor of reconstructing the history of the Chinese church. This may explain why the Chinese church historians, then and now, usually followed Western models in writing their own church history: the hagiographic-biographical genre and denominational history. Just a few examples are Luo Yanbin's *Lixianhui zai hua chuangjiaoshi* [A History of the Rhenish Mission in China, 1847–1947] (Hong Kong, 1968), Wen Guowei, *Xundao weili ru shenzhou* [Methodism in China] (Hong Kong, 1995), and Luo Feili [Philip Loh], *Xuandao yu Zhonghua: Xuandaohui zaoqi zai hua xuanjiao shilue* [Send the Doves to the Dragon: Footprints of Christian Alliance Missionaries in the Early Twentieth-Century China] (Hong Kong, 1997).

A few Christian scholars in the 1960s and 1970s, notably Lin Chih-p'ing [Peter Lin] of Taiwan and Ng Lee Ming and Jonathan Chao in Hong Kong, began to challenge the denominational lines by promoting studies on Chinese church history following Western academic models. The "Cosmic Light" [*Yu-chou-kuang*] group, under the leadership of Lin Chih-p'ing, has evolved as a socially and culturally active organization in Taiwan with considerable influence upon both Christian and non-Christian circles. After a careful perusal of the historical writings of this period — Lin Chih-p'ing's own works, Yang Shenfu's *Zhongguo jidujiao shi* [A History of Christianity in China] (Taipei, 1968), and Wei Wai-yang's *Zuanjia shiye yu jindai Zhong guo* [Missionary Enterprises and Modern China] (Taipei, 1985) — one would agree that these works were basically products of the mission history approach in which the emphasis was placed upon the missions and missionaries but not the Chinese converts. As I have confessed in the beginning of my paper, my own research in Chinese church history also began at this time with a focus on the "giving end." There were a few exceptions: Lo Hsiang-lin and Jen Yu-wen, for example, were among the very few who began to pay attention to Chinese Christians as early as the 1950s, but their work in this area was mostly ignored by others during that time.[5]

What caused the shift of focus from missions and missionary activities to indigenous leadership, church organizations, and interactions between the Chinese Christian communities and other segments of the Chinese society?

First, it grew out of an identity crisis of the Chinese Christian historians (myself included) during a time of cultural turmoil and disarray in China in the late 1960s and early 1970s. The identity crisis set off my personal journey in the late '60s in quest of the Chinese church's past. Was the Chinese church a Westernized organization as the Chinese leaders and scholars in the PRC so strongly asserted? Was Christianity a foreign religion imposed on the Chinese people? Were the missionaries collaborators with Western imperialistic governments or were they genuine helpers of the Chinese? These and other questions bothered me as a Chinese Christian intellectual in the turbulent age of revisionism and Chinese nationalism of the '60s and early '70s. For others, the process began a little earlier or sometime later. But after we began our quest, we were soon disappointed or dissatisfied by the "facelessness" and ambiguities of the Chinese in the history of Christianity in China. The role of missions and missionaries, many nevertheless acknowledged, was important in the history of Christianity in China as they were pioneers and the "Big Brother." But if the missionary was his little Chinese brother's keeper, then where was the little brother? In missionary records deposited at the home mission centers, many Chinese partners and native helpers were identity-blurred. Their full

---

5. For example, Lo Hsiang-lin had pioneered the study of Hong Kong Hakka Christians, a subject later picked up by Nichole Constable in her study of the Tsung Him Tong; see Constable, *Christian Souls and Chinese Spirits: A Hakka Community in Hong Kong* (Berkeley: University of California Press, 1994). For Jen Yu-wen, his *Zhongguo Jidujiao di kaishan shiye* [Pioneers of the Protestant Church in China] (Hong Kong: The Council on Christian Literature for Overseas Chinese, 1956) contains several biographies of early Chinese Christians.

names were rarely identified, being reduced usually to that of Mr. Wang [Wang Xiansheng], Mr. Chen [Chen Xiansheng], or simply nameless. We were not so much annoyed by the attention that the missionaries were getting at the hands of the historians as we were disturbed by the lack of information about our own predecessors. In other words, as we soon realized, there was little Chinese church history in mission history in China. The Chinese pastors, lay leaders, and colporteurs were an important part of the early Chinese church builders but have not been given due credit in mission history and in mission records. The impulse for discovering one's own roots — a common cultural phenomenon in the '70s epitomized by the popularity of the television drama series *Roots* — and a yearning for a more substantive role for the Chinese Christians in their own history, I think, became one of the important driving forces behind my own search and the search of the Christian scholars of my generation to investigate the "receiving end" of mission history.

Second, the shift came as a result of ferment in Western Sinology. As China historians in the West were attempting to break free from the "Western-centric" views — namely, the "Western Challenge–Chinese Response" paradigm, the "Modernization" paradigm, and the "Imperialism" paradigm as described in Paul Cohen's book — established by post-war "area studies" experts like John Fairbank and his students, they now paid more attention to the internal forces that shaped China's modern history. Beginning with local and regional studies (led by G. William Skinner) in the 1970s, soon the whole field of China studies became more interested in social issues that had been ignored in relation to the forces of Westernization emphasized in the past.[6] As Chinese Christian scholars, we were pleased to see this development in the field of China studies — moving away from the Western-centric paradigms — and were quick to embrace Cohen's "Chinese-centered history" approach. The Chinese church historians' emphasis on the *receiving end* and on Chinese Christians, in other words, was seen as part of the new paradigm of Chinese-centered history.

Furthermore, the gradual opening of Communist China and the increasing role played by the emerging giant in Asia also affected our research directions. We were glad to see the relaxation of political control in the academic field and an increasing number of young scholars interested in the history of Christianity

---

6. The changing trends in Western Sinology are best analyzed in Paul A. Cohen's *Discovering History in China* (1984); see chapter 4 on "China-Centered History." I have written a review article on America's historical writings on modern China analyzing the new trends, in *Zhongguo jindaishi yanjiu xinqushi* [New Trends in Modern Chinese Studies] (Hong Kong: Educational Publishers, 1994), 105–34.

in China, but we also realized they did not see the missions and missionaries in the same Christian perspectives. Their concerns and demands had to be addressed (if not followed) in an evaluation of the history of the Chinese church.

Reconstructing Chinese Church History: From Dichotomy to Joint Commitment

After we have reviewed the characteristics of mission historiography regarding China in both Chinese and English languages, we may draw some conclusions. First, we realize that mission studies in the West have been going through some fundamental changes since the late 1970s as a result of the following factors: (1) the increasing participation of secular academics in the field whose research helped alter some basic assumptions in mission history and changed the research methodology and the interpretive framework fundamentally, and (2) a new realization by missiologists and church leaders that globalization of Christianity was inaugurating a new era for Christianity in which Third World churches will play a major role.

Second, we also realize that there has been a lot of interest in the history of Christianity in China among PRC scholars due to the open-door policy of China in the Reform Era, and there has been a growing interest among Chinese Christian scholars in studying their own past by emphasizing indigenous institutions and native contributions.

As a consequence of these changing trends in Western and Chinese historiography on modern China, and in mission studies and in Chinese historiography on Christianity, the traditional distinction between mission history and Chinese church history has become blurry. Many mission studies done by secular academics now focus on Christian missions' interactions with Chinese society and culture, allowing a larger role for the native institutions and focusing more and more on local converts. Daniel Bays's "History of Christianity in China" project is a case in point. The project, developed by Bays at the suggestion of John K. Fairbank in 1984, organized two symposia in 1989 and 1990, involving thirty-some scholars from China and America. One basic theme of the project is "Christianity is here interpreted as not just a Western religion that imposed itself on China, but one that was becoming a Chinese religion." Bays calls this focus on the Chinese converts and Chinese society and Christianity becoming a Chinese religion "a process of inculturation" (1996: vii). Jessie Lutz has been moving in this direction for quite some time with her latest research on Chinese Hakka evangelists whom she calls "invisible missionaries" (Lutz and Lutz, 1995: 204–27; see Lutz, 1997).

The fusion of church history and secular academic disciplines has forced church historians and missiologists to rethink their work and their interpretations. Many of them feel that they have now come to a crossroads. Should we continue to concentrate on the research on missions? Should we adopt a "China-centered" and "Chinese-centered" approach in our studies? As Christian scholars should we keep "religion" or evangelism as an important part of our scholarly endeavor? Should we follow the methodologies of the secular academics? And as Chinese Christian historians, should we reconstruct our church history focusing on the Chinese Christians and not on the missionaries?

These questions have created a dichotomy between mission history and Chinese church history, as I have outlined in the introduction and earlier sections of this paper. And the current academic trend in Sinological studies with its "China-centered approach" only escalates the polarization — "Chinese church history" with emphasis on indigenization versus "mission history" focusing on foreign missions and missionaries. In light of the paradigmatic changes in mission history and church history, we then may ask: What constitute the components of Chinese church history? What was the role of missions and missionaries in the history of the Chinese church? Should we emphasize more the Chinese end of the story? Was Chinese Christianity a part of Western Christianity or world Christianity?

While I am an advocate of the "Chinese-centered" approach in reconstructing the history of the Christian church in China, I do not reject or look down upon mission history or mission studies like some of my fellow Chinese historians do. As a matter of fact, I have come to yet another new realization after going through first a period of studying "mission history" and then another period of advocating "Chinese church history": the two are interrelated and complementary to each other. The shift of focus in my research reflected the problem of emotional identification more than a methodological necessity in historical studies. The Chinese church, in my opinion, has owed a great deal to the pioneer work of missions and missionaries, while the missionaries themselves and the Christian mission leaders at home have also learned a great deal from the field. If we examine the interactions and interrelations between the two — field and home mission — not from the one-dimensional view of the "giver" or "spiritual and moral philanthropist," but as a reciprocal process of give-and-take, and from the view of an emerging global Christianity in which both missionaries and converts, and both the indigenous church and the home

missions, have important roles and equally significant contributions, then the
result could be mutually enriching and mutually enlightening. The sense of
rivalry and role conflict of home and field and the dilemma of dichotomy that
is embedded in the word "versus" would give way to a spirit of partnership
and a joint commitment (as the Bible says, "we are all parts of the body").
A better and sympathetic understanding of the history at both ends (that is,
a dual focus and their interconnection and interaction) would be beneficial to
all parties involved: the building and strengthening of the Chinese church, the
growth and globalization of the missions, and the expansion of God's kingdom.

In connection with "interrelatedness," I would also like to suggest two conceptual points — "interactions" and "intersections" — for further research in
the fields of mission history and Chinese church history. As I have pointed
out in the above pages, the history of missions should not be seen merely as a
one-way street: the coming of the missionaries to the China field and "giving"
to the Chinese the gospel and other Christian institutions and values. Many
missionaries had actually learned a lot from China, and in turn they became
"missionaries" of a different kind: importing Chinese culture and other things
Chinese to the West. The "giver" had become the "receiver" in this regard. And
the interaction between Western and Chinese culture in this reciprocal process
should be further studied. A recent book by Lian Xi entitled *The Conversion of
Missionaries* (1997) has explored the issue from this perspective. Another example of "interaction" between mission and field could be found in the Chinese
theological students who came to attend colleges or seminaries organized or
supported by the home church. When they returned to China, these students
became a very important part of the history of the Chinese church, but their
early experience and their work in America would have some impact on the
mission board. More importantly, the input from field could not be measured
by several individuals from the China field, but by the aggregated total of all
field workers and trainees from all over the world. From the Chinese perspective
it was only a two-way reciprocal process, but from the home mission's point
of view, it was a radial pattern, with a great number of fields converging at the
home mission as center. Looking at the history of Christianity from a Chinese
perspective would certainly miss the growth of the church in other parts of
the world. Thus mission history would provide a link or convergence to study
the radial missionary pattern. The interactions of home mission with all of the
fields definitely make the history of mission unique and different from church
history of a country or an area.

The concept of "intersections" here refers to the areas or issues that have been considered marginal in a well-defined area or discipline such as mission history or modern Chinese history. In the past, evangelical work and church planting have been the main issues in mission history, but now other issues such as the relations between missions and politics, missions and social service and philanthropy are all considered to be important issues. More recently mission colleges and mission schools in China have been a topic of popular and academic interest in China. The same thing could be said about modern Chinese history that in the past has defined itself by key political events and socioeconomic issues. Even in education, the role of mission schools and mission colleges had until recently been considered marginal. In studying the Chinese Christian women, Kwok Pui-lan has found an "intersection" between mission history and women history, and Shi Jinghuan has found a connection between cultural history and mission history in her intersectional study of the "missionary children" or "mish-kids." The traditional fields or areas are like different parts of the body while the "intersections" are like joints that link the different parts together. The Bible says Christ is the head and the different parts constitute the body which is the church. A history of the church should be inclusive, consisting of different parts of the body including the joints or "intersections." I believe that more intersectional studies between mission and the Chinese church, between church history and social and cultural history of modern China, or between missionary families and English or American China Policy, et cetera, would bring out further insights and yield good research fruits in all of the related fields.

Concluding Remarks

As we begin a new century and a new millennium, Christianity as a religion has emerged as a truly global religion. "The fact is," observes Daniel Bays, "that Christianity is now more non-Western than Western in its worldwide makeup, and the transcultural interactions and social changes that have brought that about in recent history should have compelling interest for scholars of the non-Western world" (1996: viii). Recognizing the changing nature of missions in the globalization of Christianity, many missiologists and Christian historians have been engaging in a rethinking process on mission history and mission theology. Essays by Dana L. Robert, Andrew Walls, and Gerald H. Anderson published in the *International Bulletin of Missionary Research* in recent years are only a few representatives of a much wider concerned group. In the rethinking process some have suggested radical changes. For example, Andrew Walls suggests that a "complete rethinking of the church history syllabus" is necessary in light of the global transformation of Christianity (1991: 146). Most would agree with Bays and other academic historians that the "Western-centric" approach is no longer serviceable in studying "Chinese Christianity."

In this chapter, I have chronicled the shift of interest in recent years from "Christian missions" to "Chinese church," and from the "Western-centric approaches" to "China-centered history." While my own research experience epitomized such a shift in the field, I feel that the polemics developed in the culture-conscious and race-conscious new methodologies and theories are also sometimes divisive and too apologetic. The mission history and mission studies of the nineteenth century and in the early decades of the twentieth century were products of culture and expressions of the cultural mentalities of a previous generation. We should acknowledge their limitations as well as their contributions. The new Christian history should be written from a multi-centered view of the church in different countries and regions, and should focus more on the interactions and intersections of these "hyphenated Christianities," such as "Chinese Christianity," "Indian Christianity," and "Western Christianity."

By referring frequently to personal experiences and sometimes indulging in reflective thinking, I have deviated from normal academic rules in writing this historiographical essay on the mission history of China and Chinese church history. In its earliest conception, I wanted to be dispassionate and analytical as a field historian. But the moment I started to revisit the field, the issues and the history of the Chinese church and my own struggle as a Christian to define myself as a part of the church in the Chinese cultural context demanded a role and a voice in this chapter. I have tried to accommodate both: the emotional identification of a Chinese Christian intellectual and the intellectual analysis of a trained historian. In the end I feel as if I am standing at a crossroads or an intersection — between the church and academia, and between heart and mind, wondering if my work is a product of research or part of a continuous search for self-identity.

Maybe my predicament and that of the Christian historians and missiologists who desire to find a better interpretive framework for doing new Christian history with a global perspective are not much different: both hinge on how to balance a strong Christian commitment and a high level of academic and research skills and methodologies. The major challenge for Christian historians, I think, is to integrate the two: a "Doctrine of Heart-and-Mind," to borrow a phrase from Neo-Confucianism.

— F O U R —

THE CHALLENGE OF
TEACHING CHURCH HISTORY
FROM A GLOBAL PERSPECTIVE

Gerald J. Pillay

In this chapter we move beyond the complex historiographical issues at stake to the challenge of *teaching* church history. Whatever one makes of globalization and its implications for historiography, church history, and indeed, for theology, the experiences of the classroom are sobering to say the least.

For a start, one is often faced with a generally impoverished historical awareness among undergraduates at a university — explicable partly by the unhappy experience of the study of history in schools. Partly it has to do with the diminishing value placed in several parts of the world on a sound humanities education that formerly did foster knowledge of other languages and cultures.[1] The market-relatedness of university programs in recent times tends to focus on what is immediately relevant.

Also, the place of history in the theology curriculum is not without some ambivalence. Biblical studies and systematic theology or pastoral theology (for the minister) are often rated more highly. Moreover, on the one hand, in non-Western cultures teachers have not a little difficulty explaining at times why there is as much need to study general church history as there is to study indigenous history. One has often sensed an impatience among African and Polynesian students, for example, with having to read patristic or medieval

---

1. Geoffrey Templeman, the Vice-chancellor of The University of Kent, in the Bithell Lecture over twenty years ago expressed his concern, in the context of British academic and intellectual and university life, about the "neglect of the past and the price it exacts." The Enlightenment, too, expressed a critical attitude to the past (he cites Voltaire and Gibbons as examples), but theirs was a "polished arrogance" based on a serious concern with the past. "Our rejection is more thorough going" and less insightful (Templeman, 1976, 2, 12f).

texts. On the other hand, universities in the United States under the trend of "multi-culturalism" in the last ten years have attempted to transform their prescribed list of texts in literature and history courses in order to take students beyond what is culturally and intellectually familiar. The results are patchy.

In some non-Western societies there has been a deliberate historical revisionism. In the attempt to free their culture and society from colonial and European intellectual dominance, this revisionism, sometimes consciously serving a new political purpose, is the means to restore an identity and self-determination to local communities. Ideological perspectives are presented as methodological necessities. The historical vantage point is consciously changed to that of the oppressed, the poor, the victims of unjust regimes, or the disenfranchised.

These projects have uncovered new historical insights and have discerned sources that would otherwise have gone unnoticed. While in several cases there has not been much constitutive history writing, yet there has at least been a fair amount of methodological reflection about the need for a history of the struggle for faith and freedom of the local people. It is in this context of historical affirmation of a hitherto voiceless people, where a perspectival bias is deliberate, that the case for global history has also to be made.

On the world scene, there are at least two intellectual trends that may appear at first sight to be impediments to a quest for a global perspective: the "end of history" movement and the postmodernist, post-structuralist school of thought. The former affirms the unassailability of a market-related economic arrangement within a liberal democratic frame of reference. The universalization of this economic and political dispensation, for this view, is inexorable. Sooner or later all cultures and societies, whatever their present state of evolution, will reach this goal. The only legitimate global perspective is ultimately a kind of universalized sameness. This view is extremely optimistic about the present. The latter, in principle, questions the possibility of anything that resembles a "meta-narrative." It grants validity only to the different perspectives and is skeptical of the construction of a universal that exists as an abstraction. It is imbued, not without good reasons, with skepticism and even disdain for any form of Western cultural hegemony. It is in principle anti-foundationalist and is opposed to any vital role and place for tradition. Battling the tyranny of the universal, it idolizes the perspective.

In presenting some of the historiographical challenges that are encountered in attempting to teach church history from a global perspective, I should like to offer the following observations:

1. *Teaching church history from a global perspective must include all of history. The artificial division between church history and general history makes little sense since the presupposition of a global perspective is that "the church" is a universal phenomenon. What we mean by "church history" has consequentially to be modified.*

Historical studies of any kind, whether they deal with Christian themes or not, have to meet the requirements of sound historical interpretation. This cannot be achieved if church historians limit their critical purview by neglecting interaction with other historians, and since history is a "field-encompassing field," with the other humanities and the social sciences. Religion is one of the most powerful social and cultural forces, and for long periods in both Western and non-Western societies was often the dominant influence on a society. General history cannot ignore the history of religion if it is serious about understanding the past in the same way that church historians cannot ignore general history if they are to understand the history of Christianity, its life and witness in the world. *Not only can church themes not easily be separated from other social, cultural, and political themes, but church themes are not the preserve of church historians.* This is widely evident. Some of the most illuminating work on Christian themes has been done by general historians without any obvious theological intent. The question, then, is what is the special responsibility of the church historian?

An allied concern of this first observation is the definition of church history itself, and here, too, we walk on well-traveled ground. Does *church* history in practice if not in intention not view Christian history (or rather the history of Christianity) from the perspective of the institution? In the absence of "*the* church" as an easily defined entity, still less as a discernible entity, what in fact are we studying in church history? Can the historian assume a meaning of "church" that in reality is difficult to discern and which the churches themselves have difficulty explaining? Can the historian contrive a unity that in practice may have been non-existent, at least for long periods of church history? This lack of a common ecclesial vision within Christianity is especially acute after the period of the Seven Ecumenical Councils and the schism between the Latin West and the Greek East. In spite of the struggle for a common faith, in this period there was at least the making of a common ecclesial mind that became impossible after 1054 and which modern ecumenism in its myriad forms is still far from resolving.

Speaking of "the history of Christianity" or of the "Christian movement" appears to move beyond merely the institutional perspective or the conglomerate story of the histories of the different churches. However, the history of Christianity can sometimes be too wide for those who seek to understand the "ecclesial mind" and the interpretive tradition that links the earliest Christian communities with the long and diverse history of Christian churches and communities. Christian influence is found outside the churches as well; in law, social forms, morality, art, and in all those facets of life that are not always qualified by the word "Christian." Furthermore, a *social* history of the church is a necessary but not a sufficient domain for church historians. It, in any case, does not require any special skills unavailable to general historians.

2. *A global perspective is obviously spatial in that it takes seriously the fact that Christianity is now a multiracial, multinational, and multicultural phenomenon.*

The fact of globalization is what is recognized here. Christianity has a worldwide cultural and social presence. The sixteenth-century Catholic mission presented the first clear signs that Christianity could permanently burst its Mediterranean and mainly European geographical boundaries, which it had had for almost fifteen hundred years. This was in spite of the numerous attempts to do so before this period: the early Christian presence in India, Armenia, and China, for example. The Protestant missionary expansion of the nineteenth century, more widespread and more culturally diverse, made this new global reality forever explicit. The case is graphically and simply made in the classroom by comparisons of maps showing the extension of Christianity from its inception to the present. It quickly becomes clear how relatively narrow a geographic existence Christianity mainly had until about the eighteenth century. Culturally and geographically it has covered more ground in the last two hundred years than it had in the previous eighteen hundred years.

The World Missionary Conference of 1910 brought to bear on the Christian consciousness the extent and implications of this world status of Christianity. Although William Carey had hoped that a meeting of this kind would be held in Cape Town a hundred years earlier, it only became possible at the end of the first decade of the twentieth century, after a century of experience with non-European cultures. It is noteworthy that the architects and chief organizers of this conference were missionaries who had been immersed in non-Western cultures (Noll, 1996: 51–62).[2] Even the well-intentioned supporters

---

2. Mark Noll, among others, has shown to what extent historians are indebted to missiologists for understanding how both from a vantage point of the extension of Christianity and from the aspect of the missionaries' intercultural perspectives an ecumenical history is possible. "As *Christian* interpreters," says Noll, "missiologists provide the perspectives whereby historians

of mission "abroad" had to be reeducated into seeking out the implications of taking the Christian message to the ends of the earth for Christianity itself. The extension itself had implications for its nature (Gassmann, 1995: 43–44).[3]

We are dealing here, however, with more than geography at two levels. First, the emergence of "the global village" and the ability in contemporary culture to connect nations and cultures across the globe in a remarkably short time has introduced unprecedented communication and social contact between hitherto isolated peoples. The point of significance for our purposes is that we cannot interpret these cultures as if they will be recognizable in their present forms for long. Second, besides this openly discernible interdependence between nations that came in the wake of the global village, a shift has occurred in the center of gravity of Christianity from its traditional moorings in the West to what has been termed the "Two-Thirds" World where Christianity has made its main numerical advances and where the majority of Christians now reside. In 1961, E. H. Carr, for example, in his George Macaulay Trevelyan Lectures at Cambridge, pointed out that "After some four hundred years the world center of gravity has definitely shifted from Western Europe." He added, "It is by no means clear that the world center of gravity now resides, or will continue to reside, in the English-speaking world with its Western annex. It appears to be the great land-mass of Eastern Europe and Asia, with its extensions into Africa, which today calls the tune in world affairs" (Carr, 1986: 142). He naturally had in mind a global sociopolitical shift. In just thirty-five years, much of that historian's "prophecy" has been fulfilled and much already outdated (Barraclough, 1955: 204, 217–20, 2).[4]

---

are preserved from the blood lust of ideology (a characteristic of the pre-modern period), the desiccation of scientific pretense (a modernist characteristic), and the silence of deconstructive solipsism (a postmodernist predicament)" (1996: 62). Missiologists, he adds, are in the best position to relativize the ideological, scientific, and postmodern while sharing their strong points since they, he claims, "already have learned to balance the perspectives of various cultures and to explore the shape of Christian contextualization in a variety of widely scattered regions" (1996: 51).

3. Gunter Gassmann reminds us that this "realization" of the worldwide orientation was typically achieved with the help of secular powers. "The global context," he says, "was often conceived and realized in a manner that in the analysis of later generations was marked by limitations and distortions" (43–44).

4. Geoffrey Barraclough spoke in 1955 of the "end of European history" in the sense that "end" means to cease to have the same historical significance, which, ipso facto, must mean for the whole world. The idea of "global" had not yet passed into common parlance. By "significance" he meant the significance it had in the previous eight hundred or nine hundred years. He points out, "it may be argued that Europe still remains the center of the world; but its position is reversed. Instead of being a center from which energy and initiative radiated outward, Europe

Spatial extension, then, more than merely geographic extension, includes a new sense of interconnectedness and interdependence between peoples that was quite unthinkable before the twentieth century. This process was accompanied by a shift in the center of gravity from West to East and North to South. While these shifts may still be contended by political historians, they are fairly self-evident when reviewing the history of Christianity at the beginning of this century. Not only has there been a transmutation between "mainstream" and "marginal" when it comes to Western and non-Western Christianity, but this realignment has occurred *within* non-Western societies as well. There are instances where traditional denominations that constituted the mainstream are in fact becoming increasingly marginal. Certain indigenous forms of Christian churches, which hitherto were studied by way of one or another sociological theory as historians were wont to do when dealing with the unfamiliar, are now numerically and culturally the stronger (Pillay, 1988: 125–35). Thus global shifts are sometimes mirrored in shifts within local societies. The African-initiated churches are a good example of how within South African society their growth and numbers of churches make them the single largest religious group. With the decline in the growth of the traditional denominations, what is mainstream and what is marginal has to be reevaluated.[5] These hitherto marginal communities, in a remarkably short time, also pursue the recovery of their history, for on it depends their legitimacy within the broader society and within the Christian family. Sheldrake points out that

> As new groups emerge into self-consciousness or those which have been marginalized recover their sense of identity (for example, the indigenous Christians of Latin America or the laity in the church), they demand not only a present but also a history.... In general terms, one of the effects of this approach to history has been to emphasize its complexity and variety and to question the older, chronological or narrative approach. (1992: 18)

---

has become a center upon which non-European energy and initiative converge, but even this is changing....Asia [through] sheer demographic weight may become the dominant factor and in no far distant time leave Europe in a backwash" (204, 217–20). "Every age," he concludes, "needs its own view of history and today we need a new view of the European past, adapted to the new perspectives in which the old Europe stands in a new age of global politics and global civilization" (2).

5. It is estimated that there are over 3000 African-initiated churches in South Africa alone with a membership in excess of 10 million. The total population of South Africa is around 40 million, and about 77 percent claim Christian affiliation.

If left at the level of geography and spatiality, however, a global perspective can become merely the adding on of the histories of the new churches and new expressions of Christianity to the body of historical knowledge we have of traditional forms of Christianity (Tucker, 1992: 23).[6] Global history becomes a kaleidoscope or collage, at best the presentation of a grand multi-cultural and multi-racial picture, at worst another attempt by the first and second worlds to initiate and determine the painting of the grand canvass. Many former marginal communities, who struggle to determine first their *own* history and who have sought room to be able to recover their own stories, are not primarily concerned at this stage with painting the whole picture.

Gonzalez, for instance, warns of this implication for our quest when he points out that he himself had encouraged some form of globalization for almost thirty years, yet he agrees with S. M. Heim's "suspicion that globalization is an ideal formulated by Westerners in such a way that they alone have the means to be experts at it." He adds, "Theirs is a form of 'globalization' that, even if its proponents do not realize it, is one more way in which the West imposes standards on the rest of the world, and then faults them for not meeting such standards" (1993: 49). He laments that in countries like the United States, the problems of marginality and social disinheritance often exist unnoticed in one's "own backyard."

The Enlightenment's quest for a "universal history" assumed a certain configuration of world cultures and societies. Their characterization was determined by certain presuppositions about the place and role of European societies and cultures in the scheme of things. In retrospect, it is quite understandable how these typologies of world cultures would be biased, since those constituting them were part and parcel of European cultures and scholarship. This quest for a universal history led to disciplines such as anthropology, sociology, political science, and history itself pursuing a deeper understanding of non-European cultures. Nevertheless, while removing myths about these cultures, these disciplines often functioned on the basis of these very typologies of world cultures. Tang, for example, points out that disciplines such as anthropology represented the world in a

> comprehensive typology of ethnocentrically constructed, evaluated, and reified space.... Deeply indebted to the Enlightenment vision of univer-

---

6. In this approach to writing an ecumenical history, writes Ruth Tucker, one "simply adds another 100 pages to fit in all the rest": the history of women, minorities, and other cultures (1992: 23).

sal history, this new discipline diligently attempted to classify human societies across the world.... Societies that have not adopted or participated in progressive historical time are labeled "people without a history" whereas the "hot" historical societies, in Europe and white America, are believed to be the sole possession of the future of humanity. (1996: 231)

If we are to take seriously these other cultures, then the idea of "homogenous time" becomes obsolete. Postmodernists such as Derrida speak of a "decentering" when describing the process of decolonizing European thought, whereby European culture ceases to consider itself as "the culture of reference."

What is of methodological value in this "cultural reservation" is that it would not do to conceive of creating a global perspective by placing alongside of each other the numerous histories of the different faith traditions and cultural communities: a kind of parallel reading of church history with new chapters now written to incorporate non-Western histories of the churches or histories of non-Western churches. Since the historian cannot have a God's-eye view of history, where is the historian standing in a phenomenological collage of this kind? Also, should not the case move beyond the mental attitude of the historian, beyond just the issues of fair-mindedness and equal space for all, to exploring what the methodological significance is of acquiring a global perspective? The achievement of a global perspective must surely mean more than an international and intercultural dialogue, but includes a critical dialogue between the different perspectives — a process that invariably leads to self-criticism as well. Richard Norris asks that over and above the acquisition of new perspectives there should be the possibilities to actually take some of the results of the other perspective seriously and be influenced by them (1995: 24f).

Latourette in his own work earlier in this century had broadened this spatial dimension of the global to include all of humanity. In his introduction to *A History of Christianity* in 1953, he wrote,

> Since Christians have claimed that Christ is essential to a comprehension of the meaning of history, since the outlook of Christianity is universal in its scope, and since from the outset the ideal has been set before the followers of Jesus of winning all persons to his discipleship, the historian must ask how far that understanding and that dream have been realized. The historian's canvass, therefore, must be all humankind from the beginning to the present. (xvi–xvii)

The agnostic Benedetto Croce wrote much earlier that

> The...whole of humanity is not present to itself, and has no being
> except in the making of it, and the making is never in general, but a
> determinate and historical task. Therefore, in the accomplishment of
> that task, humanity expresses itself in its wholeness. (1941: 280)

The question must be raised in the context of the theme of these essays as
to how *effective* cooperative attempts at the synthesis of history can be. The
Ecclesiastica Historia led by Flacius Illyricus and four other directors, with two
architectes and seven *studiosi,* attempted to present "global" annalistic history in
1554 and included non-Christian religious thinking as well. This erudite work
is as "dead as mutton," writes F. M. Powicke (1955: 201)[7] while Gibbon's
Decline and Fall he considers to be *effective* because it "lives." He believed that
those "who carried on the work of the Maurists in France and organized the
Monumenta in Germany chose the right way. Their history, written in solitude
with deep searchings of mind and spirit, was all the better because they were
also taking the lead in the co-operative tasks" (ibid.: 202). He adds, "any
amount of cooperation in the synthesis of history remains to be done. How
can it be made most effective?" This for us, too, is a crucial question!

The whole human story, however, is not an abstraction created by the historian but obtains
in the intensity with which the constituent parts are taken seriously. This quest to tell
the whole human story or more particularly the story of the integration of
Christianity within the whole human story includes the perspectives of which
general historians have reminded us regarding the dimensions of life beyond
institutions, national aspirations, and political systems. They have highlighted
what should have been commonsensical: the need for family, personal, and communal history — the fabric of human life in its fullest sense. Crucial to the
understanding of the whole Christian story is the history of ordinary people, of
worship and worshiping communities, of life and thought, of Christian morality and spirituality, and not, as the case has so often been, of mainly synods
and doctrinal development. The late S. Immanual David of India reminded us,

> When theologians speak of the church as the people of God, they often
> mean by this the *whole* body. The differences between classes, between rich
> and poor, between educated and illiterate, are not the center of interest.

---

7. *The Cambridge Histories, Ancient, Indian, Modern and Imperial,* a great cooperative venture to
which Powicke himself contributed, is no more effective in its synthesis, he concludes. It stands
halfway between "real history and an encyclopedia" (202).

But historians of the present generation use the word "people" in such a way that those differences are also audible. "People," then, is almost equivalent to "ordinary people" i.e. denoting those without power, the oppressed, the poor. Nearly 80 percent of the Christian community in India is made up of such people. (1988: 107)

This statistic is true for Africa as well!

This concern is not valid just for globally far-flung communities today but even more so for those that have existed before our time. How often those of us confronted with the task of making accessible to our students the early Christian communities have struggled to gain simple information about them as people; their aspirations and their hopes and doubts as believers; their worship and their communal, family, and social life. Yet so much is available on the doctrinal controversies, the establishment of early Christian institutions and offices, and the church's public role after the Edict of Milan. While one must not overlook the complexity of the task of uncovering this history of the broader community — this communal history — the fact that it is so infrequently attempted by church historians relative to their pursuit of the history of the institutions and dogma is an indication of how their interests have tended to be one-dimensional.

This is not a new communal concern (highlighted in our times by those wishing to interpret Christianity in the Third World). What has come to be known as a "history from below," which passed into common usage among historians after Edward Thompson's article by that name in 1966, came to be possible about 1788, as Eric Hobsbawn has pointed out, with the history of mass movements in the eighteenth century (Sharpe, 1991: 25f). Jim Sharpe concludes, "We must admit, regretfully, that although the concept has been with us for over two decades, history from below has so far had comparatively little impact on mainstream history or on altering the perspectives of mainstream historians" (ibid.: 37). The task is to extend this communal reading of history back some two thousand years and to resist the tendency to separate thought from the life of communities, belief and action from worldview and from cultural change and continuity.

3. *A global historical perspective provides the indispensable time dimension that brings to bear on the spatial, "the long view."*

It sounds trite to speak of history having a time dimension but in the quest to make church history "inclusive," one of the difficulties is to justify to students why, for example, the histories of premodern, medieval, and early Greek Christian communities have any relevance at all. Or if we are going to study earlier Christian views, should their relevance be assessed only insofar as they have something to say directly to our communities and their problems? Not to heed to this historical "Marcionite" prescription is to impose — it is sometimes claimed — a form of historicism or, at worst, "Eurocentrism."

Whatever the present ideological mood governing the historical process, and there is a view that treats ideology not only as a positive but also as a desirable and indispensable qualifier to meaningful historical writing, in the absence of the long view, the church historian has no real basis to assess what in Christian history has limited or lasting significance. Ultimately, if church history is to be faithful to its hermeneutical responsibility (and this is what distinguishes it from history in general), it is this long view that provides a meaningful grasp of the tradition in which a trend or theological position can best be assessed. Interim trends or theological fashions and too hasty judgments about "paradigm shifts" and such are relativized only against the backdrop of the interpretive process that goes back to the earliest texts on which Christian life and thought derive their meaning and to the history of the interpretation of these texts. As G. R. Elton stated it,

> An individual experience, of course, is always limited and commonly dis-
> torted by prejudice and self-interest: what men and women need is an
> enlarged experience against which to measure the effect of these disad-
> vantages. That experience is made available by the historian presenting
> the past in all its variety and potential, and all of it divorced from the
> immediate needs and concerns of the present (1991: 72).[8]

What we are particularly concerned with here is the hermeneutical link that Christian history has with the Apostolic tradition. Here is the critical rub: a large part of Protestant scholarship pays little or no regard to any continuity with Apostolic tradition and indeed sometimes argues to jettison this tradition.

---

8. Brian Stock has argued that there has been a "general neglect of tradition among social scientists," who have, since the Enlightenment, used it as an opposite of "change." Tradition has come to mean the "culturally changeless and historically immobile" (1990: 159f). Tradition, in his view, is what gives history a sense of "overarching unity"; it has "authoritative presence" and is not only *traditum* but also *traditio*: that which helps to shape what is being transmitted. The works of S. N. Eisenstadt, *Tradition, Change and Modernity* (New York, 1993); J. C. Heesterman, *The Inner Conflict of Tradition*, studies in Indian history and society; E. Shils, *Tradition*; and Pelikan, *The Vindication of Tradition* are some examples of historians attempting to set right this impoverished attitude toward tradition.

The difficulty then is that the historical view is greatly shortened, based on a set of eighteenth-century presuppositions (Robinson, 1920: 252).

Yet, the largest part of the Christian family is from cultures that did not go through the fragmentation of the Western worldview that came in the wake of the so-called "Enlightenment" and its concomitant secularization. They do not neatly distinguish between the sacred and the secular.

One may argue in the fashion of the "end of history" school that this fragmentation is inevitable or that these cultures are premodern and, perhaps, even prescientific and that the universality of liberal democracy and a market-related economy will inexorably be the leveler. But this line of argument underscores not only the Eurocentrism of the position but also the depth with which this view is modernist in a new guise.

Norris has made the point that

> If it is the business of historians to establish a real communication with the past, even a tentative and perhaps superficial communication, one would have to see evidence in their writings that the past does not always respond amiably when the "lively issues" of the present dominate the conversion. . . . It is not until the past shrugs its shoulders with indifference that one can be reasonably sure that communication is actually taking place. (1995: 32–33)

Gadamer, probably more than anyone else in the twentieth century, has shown how indeed all interpretive activity is done within a tradition and is in service to this tradition. Even when the interpretation questions the tradition, the very questioning leads to the enrichment of the tradition; he describes incisively the "hermeneutical circle" that exists between the interpreted textual history and the nature of the ongoing transmutation of presuppositions (or "prejudices," as he puts it) in the interpreter. At the point of achieving an understanding of the past, the tradition is also extended. His is not an argument for historicism or for the conservative clinging to traditions at all cost, but a clear description of the interpretive process that the historian and all interpreters are part of.

It is not a Christian philosophy of history that is meant here, but an interpretive frame of reference with which to make sense of Christian life and thought and its multicultural and multinational forms. In the absence of an interpretive frame of reference (that is, agreement as to what constitutes the Christian tradition), the historian sails rudderless. Christian history becomes the history of *everything* and while the compilation of the Christian compendium running into many tomes will no doubt bear all the marks of erudition and be an important resource, its theological responsibility will still be left unattended. The question of what constitutes the *Christian* tradition will have to be dealt with later if not sooner. This is especially a Protestant ecclesiological dilemma. A global perspective for church history that takes seriously the history of the Catholic and Orthodox churches and includes the churches of the Third World can hardly be possible while this dilemma is unresolved.

But there is another methodological consideration that requires this long view: namely, the basis by which historical choices can be made about facts and sources in presenting a story so far-reaching in both width and depth. These choices are made on the basis of what the historian considers of lasting historical significance and what is pivotal. In his inaugural lecture, Butterfield cautioned that "great history may turn on a small pivot, so that rather than trying to study all the details, it may be better to hunt for the pivotal detail" (1965: 24).[9]

> 4. *Christianity in a global perspective is ecumenical, but all ecumenical history is not necessarily global.*

It is at this level of the question that the matter of ecclesiology or, to state it differently, the theological focus of what constitutes "Christianity" is most crucial. Even telling the story, for example, of the proliferation of Protestantism since the sixteenth century, if it is not merely to be the record of the institutional breakaways and a cold description of strife, must reflect the theological integrity of each group if it is to explain the reason for the proliferation. Inversely, the telling of the story of sixteenth-century church history requires a theological frame of reference not only to explain the proliferation but to make sense of the influences each group had on the other, an aspect often neglected in the "oppositional" way these schisms are dealt with. It is in understanding the influences and the theological stumbling blocks to a common understanding of the Faith that some semblance of an ecumenical history emerges. H. G. Wells acknowledged something similar in the introduction to *The Outline of History*. He writes,

---

9. To illustrate, Butterfield adds, "It makes the mind reel to think of trying to calculate all the history that would have to be rewritten and all the deep structure of things that might have been altered if in 1789 there had been a man like Henri IV instead of Louis XVI on the French throne. And even in the twentieth century, it might have been effectively a small handful of men, who, because they had faith in what they were doing, produced in 1917 what within thirty years had come to appear as one of the greatest landslides in human history" (24).

There can be no peace now, we realize, but a common peace; no prosperity but a general prosperity. But there can be no common peace and prosperity without common historical ideas. Without such ideas to hold them together in harmonious co-operation, with nothing but narrow, selfish, and conflicting nationalist traditions, races and peoples are bound to drift toward conflict and destruction (in Williams, 1938: 109).[10]

The equivalent of these "connecting historical ideas" for the church historian is the ecclesial frame of reference, *open enough to make sense of the expanding understanding of the Christian message and of Christian self-understanding, but lucid enough to be able to discern the shared heritage (the common story) without lapsing into the story of Everything.*

In a sense, Christian communities from the very beginning attempted to be both ecumenical and global. They sought to maintain their unity in spite of grave difficulties and theological struggles. But at the same time, they also believed that the gospel was for the *oecumene*, and under the mandate of Christ, they took their faith to the "whole inhabited world" (the then-known world). Their faith in that sense was also global, given the geographic extent of the Christian faith by the time of the schism of 1054 or even at the time of the rise of Protestantism. As the geographic boundaries were pushed back, the Christian message also spread. When the whole globe became known, these Christians were among the first to carry their message now literally "to the uttermost parts of the earth." While the Christian message has always in this sense been global, it became less and less ecumenical. One of the ironies is that at the time of the most far-reaching Western "discoveries" of global societies and cultures, Christianity (especially the Protestant branch) began its proliferation. Now we are faced with the fact that Christianity is a global religion with transcultural and transnational constituencies, but is by no means an ecumenical whole.

There is a sense in which ecumenical history is the attempt to transcend the divisions between Christian denominations. It seeks not merely to trace the attempts at Christian unity but seeks an alternative way of presenting the history of these Christian traditions. Gassmann defines ecumenical history as the attempt to understand "those efforts and movements within Christian or

---

10. In this introduction Wells also states regarding the narrating of a world history that "many topics of quite primary interest to mankind, the first appearance and the growth of scientific knowledge, for example, and its effects upon human life, the elaboration and ideas of money and credit, or the story of the origins and spread of Christianity, which must be treated fragmentarily or by elaborate digressions in any partial history, arise and flow completely and naturally in one general record of the world in which we live."

church history whose aim is to overcome divisions among Christians . . . and to bring them to forms of communion that will enable them to confess together the one apostolic faith, to live with each other in spiritual communion" (1995: 40). It involves, as G. R. Evans points out, the process whereby one overcomes revisionism by "purifying memory"; it is liberated from not having a common history and yet enriched by having a shared heritage, not merely forgetting but accepting the ambiguities as well (1994: 93f).

Ecumenical history also attempts to tell the story of the church by telling the story of the churches and of Christian movements, which confronts not only the lack of homogeneity but is vitally interested in the connections and in the shared heritage. The "connections" may be the result of conscious attempts at unity or fellowship between churches but may also include those groups that have no interest in formal fellowship, but whose life and thought resemble parts of the Christian family in spite of cultural and contextual differences. The lack of homogeneity obtains simply in the fact that alongside the familiar linear story of Christianity, that traces the present to Palestine through mainly western Europe, were Christian communities in Africa and Asia as well; the latter, while not being numerically significant, embody an old Christian tradition and ethos. This historical search for the connecting tradition is an important prolegomenon to any attempt to tell the whole story.[11] Global history, we must assume, is ecumenical history in this sense. It has to do with more than providing equitable space in the one story but deals with "the whole Christian church on earth" (Gassmann, 1995: 4).[12]

5. *Historiographically speaking, the particular is connected to the whole, the local to the global, and the contextual to the catholic.*

The Project on Christian History in Ecumenical Perspective[13] presented as one of fourteen principles for an ecumenical history the following: "An ecumenical history of Christianity is global in outlook and seeks to avoid geographic centrism, classicism, ethnocentrism, sexism, and the cult of per-

---

11. Dale Irwin (1991) warns there is no "master narrative" in this venture.

12. Gassmann reminds us that this description of the subject of church history is from Luther's Small Catechism (4).

13. This working group comprised representatives from twenty-four churches (Protestant, Orthodox, Catholic, and independent churches) that emerged in the U.S. Its fourteen principles appear in the essay "Christian History in Ecumenical Perspective: Principles of Historiography," in T. J. Wengert and C. W. Brockwell, eds. (1995).

sonality" (Wengert and Brockwell, 1995: 5). In his reaction to this principle, Norris makes the point that

> Feminist treatments of Christian history can scarcely be labeled "global in outlook," yet none would deny their utility or their ability to bring forgotten tracts of history to light. Neither the J Document, nor recent studies in black religion in Africa and the Americas, nor the new birth of Latin American church history can be acquitted of a certain "ethnocentricism." ... [I]f the fourth century Arian historian Philostorgius were with us, it would doubtless be necessary to add "homousianism" to the above list of forbidden delights. But why forbid them if they contribute to knowledge and understanding? (1995: 24)

If the quest for a global perspective in the classroom is to go beyond merely what constitutes an acceptable moral attitude in the historian toward the numerous sectors that are studied, it would have to deal with the methodological issue that is raised here concerning what the relation is between local, contextual, and cultural histories and a global history.[14]

Butterfield, in his inaugural address, lamented that in spite of the internationalism that had clearly set in by the middle of the twentieth century, historiography was still "colored by nationality" which fostered "insularity." "The insular approach," he added, "produces not merely nationalistic bias but a more general intellectual constriction that is even less easy to detect in oneself. At the highest level it impoverishes — it reduces by a whole dimension — that mental background from which our hypotheses and hunches so mysteriously emerge" (1965: 13). He is not seeking to diminish the local here in favor of the global but argues that the global is crucial for the understanding of national history. He writes, "Though we ourselves [he means here 'the English'] might seem to have a special justification for being insular, there could hardly be a better example than England for illustrating how even one's own domestic

---

14. "Their mirror is shattered," writes Marc Ferro. "Universal history is dead; it died from being a European mirage which reflected Europe's own illusions as to her own destiny" (1984: ch. 15). He maintains that there are two different "centers": "institutional history" and "societies' memories," which is not history in the sense of the academy. He warns against "grinding out" a universal history from a single center that could be an act of "tyranny." The question remains whether what he sees as "institutional history" did not begin at some stage as the memory of "individuals and collectives" before a literary tradition emerged among them and before these people themselves began to reflect on their history and write it down. It seems that the writer perceives that this stage can be preserved in cultural and intellectual isolation today.

history cannot properly be studied in isolation. We do not always realize what we owe to repeated blood-transfusions from the continent" (ibid.: 14).[15]

The inter-relatedness between the whole and the particular is endemic to the historical process and cannot be presented to students as alternatives or as mutually exclusive, no matter where one is teaching. The pursuit of a contextual reading is as crucial to uncovering perspectives and sources that would otherwise go unnoticed as the need to ask what the global or catholic implication of that perspective is. The integrity of the local or contextual perspective lies, says Cyril Powles, in the difference between proselytism and conversion. He points out that when the Christians in the first century rejected circumcision they were rejecting proselytism, whereby they would become part of the Jewish race so that they may become Christians. "In its place they recognized that the grace of God could act to call forth the response of metanoia . . . *within* their own cultural context" (1984: 138). Conversion, then, is a far more "indigenous" and thoroughgoing process of cultural immersion than proselytization.

The global and the local are mirrored in the relation between what is catholic and the contextual. Each new context highlights a new dimension of the gospel by virtue of the fact that it puts a new question to the text and the Christian tradition. It draws from the text a new facet, implicit but hitherto uncovered. Each new context plumbs the depth of the informing text and extends the tradition as the gospel emerges uniquely in each new context. These new facets are in no danger of becoming parochial or "tribal" or even heretical because this interpretive process can only take place meaningfully in solidarity to a tradition outside of which it is purposeless. We may say that *for the gospel to be truly catholic, it has to be "contextualized" everywhere.* As *Lumen Gentium* states it, "The local or particular churches are no longer seen as subordinate and only partial expressions of the universal church, but in them and formed out of them the one and unique Catholic church exists." F. C. Baur illustrated this interconnection between the local and the universal in historical theology when he wrote,

> The phases of dogma in the course of its temporal development show how dogma repeatedly represents a new form and aspect to the consciousness

---

15. E. J. Hobsbawn illustrates this interdependency in historiography by showing how the local and communal experience of the Civetello della Chiana at the hands of the German army was as vital for historians as the holocaust for the Jewish people (1994: 53). Similarly, the experience at Sharpeville is as important for those who lived in that African location in Johannesburg in the 1950s as it is for making sense of South African history over three hundred years.

of each respective age, so that the whole history of dogma is to be conceived as a development, indeed infinitely manifold yet nevertheless thoroughly organic, of the one Christian consciousness, determined by the necessity of the subject matter.... Likewise, the universal and the particular cannot be related to each other externally; rather, the particular and the special can be understood only as the concrete manifestation of the universal. (1968: 318)

Recently, Shenk (1996) in his "Toward a Global Church History," while affirming the indispensability of the local and the contextual, is forthright about the "assumption that what happened in the West cannot be universally normative for Christian history," also makes the point that "The writing of authentic non-Western church history does not by itself fulfill the vision of a global church history.... [E]ach of these encouraging developments over the last fifty years has made an important contribution but is only a partial corrective" (1996: 54). He adds, "The people of Christ can no longer afford to live in the era of Western or any other parochialism" (ibid.: 56). Writing from a completely different vantage point, E. J. Hobsbawn argues in the same vein: "All human collectives necessarily are or have been part of a larger more complex world" (1994: 63). A history written only for a collective out of loyalty may be "comforting" but is not good history. As an end in itself it is "dangerous. The sentences typed on apparently innocuous keyboards may be sentences of death" (ibid.: 63).[16] The critical tension between the global and the local is what ensures contextual relevance but at the same time prohibits local interests from becoming exaggerated. The threat of insularity is as real as the threat of abstraction.[17]

In the classroom, it is not possible to teach everything or adequately teach the history of world Christianity except in outline. I come back to the question

---

16. I mentioned Jim Sharpe's concern about "history from below" having no influence on the mainstream. He adds, however, in the next paragraph that this history from below "however valuable should...be brought out of the ghetto (or peasant village, working class street, slum) and used to criticize, redefine and strengthen the historical mainstream" (38). There seems to be strong consensus among a broad range of scholars representing quite different theological concerns for the interdependence between the local and the global.

17. Geoffrey Barraclough in his presidential address to the History Society on its Diamond Jubilee cited what his predecessor at the University of Liverpool had said to illustrate the danger of this kind of historical myopia: "No one surveying the minute investigations conducted by English historians into the details of English constitutional practice in the reign of Henry III could possibly realize that the great issue of the day was whether Europe would be submerged by the Mongol hordes" (1967: 8).

raised earlier about where the historian stands in the process. After all, most of our students will in the main end up living in the same part of the world for all their lives. What is crucial is that while immersed in their contexts they are able to place their lives and their thoughts in global perspective; that they grasp the catholic dimension of their contextual witness and thus are able to enrich the Christian tradition. This in the end may be the most important benefit from grasping the global perspective.

FIVE

WORLD CHRISTIANITY AND THE NEW HISTORIOGRAPHY

History and Global Interconnections

Lamin Sanneh

Old and New Historiography

History, Lord Acton once said, is not a web woven by innocent hands, though, by the same token, he contends it is the true demonstration of religion. History, he insists, is not the infallible voice of God in men and women, but it is not a moral amnesty either, for it does not allow us to make exceptions, to tinker with weights and measures, and to espouse the positivist dogma that whatever exists is right and reasonable, a position that makes a religion out of fashion. A certain moral tension, at least, would thus seem to animate the historical craft.

When it concerns the subject of this study, history is not a national or racial monopoly, nor even the monopoly of the victors, though the victors have had the lion's share of representing history. It is a fact of some historical import that vanquished groups are entitled to be considered better than mere throw-away objects of historical inevitability because their cause does touch on our own interests. In that connection we may recall Acton's observation that "the footsteps of a silent but prophetic people who dwelt by the Dead Sea, and perished in the fall of Jerusalem, come nearer to our lives than the ancestral wisdom of barbarians who fed their swine on the Hercynian acorns" (Fears, 1988: 519). The historian's business here is to do the best for the other side which is the underside, to resist the force of the West's claims to primacy and instead take the pathways of those unofficial agents, such as catechists, teachers, nurses, exhorters, evangelists, and translators, who took responsibility for church planting. This underdog sentiment is aptly expressed in Bob Marley's popular reggae song, "By the Waters of Babylon."

As a general matter, then, historical evidence and its interpretation are interdependent, united in the single goal of joining act and intention, fact and appreciation, of taking hold of a dead past and bringing it within range of our own life and work. In the particular matter of the subject of this study, however, past grievances are especially susceptible to vigilant touchiness, or equally to guilt-laden defensiveness. At any rate, the subject is not a matter of indifference, even if it still remains insulated from mainstream academic discourse.

Mission History and a World Upside Down

To turn now to the historiography of mission and world Christianity, in his *History of Christian Missions,* Stephen Neill (1964a: 15) describes how Christianity has emerged from its Asiatic confinement and found a home in nearly every country in the world, with followers among all races and without regard to civilized or primitive criteria. He quotes Archbishop William Temple (1881–1944) to the effect that what Neill called "this great worldwide Christendom, the result in the main of the Christian missionary work of the last two and a half centuries" became, in Temple's words, "the great new fact of our time." Neill then asked pointedly, "How is it that a religion of the Middle East radically changed its character by becoming the dominant religion of Europe, and is now changing its character again through becoming a universal religion, increasingly free from the bounds of geography and of Western civilization?" (ibid.).

Neill's observation that oriental geography and European culture had even in his day ceased to define Christianity had been stated in a less direct way by Kenneth Scott Latourette in his multivolume *History of Christianity* (1953) — the brief word was never Latourette's weakness — to be distinguished from another encyclopedic work of his, *The History of the Expansion of Christianity* in seven volumes. Latourette writes in his *History of Christianity* as follows:

> In the relatively brief nineteen and a half centuries of its existence, in spite of its seemingly unpromising beginning, Christianity had spread over most of the earth's surface and was represented by adherents in almost every tribe and nation and in nearly every inhabited land. It had gone forward in pulsations of advance, retreat, and advance. Measured by the criteria of geographic extent, inner vigor as shown by new movements from within it, and the effect on mankind as a whole, each major advance carried it further into the life of the world than the one before it and each

major recession had been less severe than its predecessor. (Latourette, 1953: 1468)

Latourette asks at the end of his *History* about the meaning and end of history. He had dropped enough hints in earlier pages to prepare the reader for his answer to that question. Using a combination of the moral teachings of Jesus and the deeds and actions of people inspired by those moral teachings, Latourette affirms the following:

> The ideal and the goal have determined the character of the [historical] movements which have been the fruits of Christianity. Although men can use and often have used knowledge and education to the seeming defeat of the ideal, across the centuries Christianity has been the means of reducing more languages to writing than have all the other factors combined. It has created more schools, more theories of education, and more systems than has any other one force. More than any other power in history it has impelled [human beings] to fight suffering, whether that suffering has come from disease, war, or natural disasters. It has built thousands of hospitals, inspired the emergence of nursing and medical professions, and furthered movements for public health and the relief and prevention of famine. Although explorations and conquests which were in part its outgrowth led to the enslavement of Africans for the plantations of the Americas, men and women whose consciences were awakened by Christianity and whose wills it nerved brought about the abolition of Negro slavery. Men and women, similarly moved and sustained, wrote into the laws of Spain and Portugal provisions to alleviate the ruthless exploitation of the Indians of the New World.... The list might go on indefinitely. It includes many another humanitarian project and movement, ideals in government, the reform of prisons and the emergence of criminology, great art and architecture, and outstanding literature. In geographic extent and potency the results were never as marked as in the nineteenth and twentieth centuries. (Ibid.: 1470–71)

"What meaning does this history of Christianity have?" Latourette asks again (ibid.). In a sense, Latourette asks the question because he has prepared the answer, and that answer, he says, need not contradict the facts ascertained by observation and appraised by human reason. In any event, the answer comes finally as an act of faith based on a study of the records of the Christian story. Yet it is clear that Latourette has applied a cultural and civilizational test to the undisputed success of Christianity, not the plurality of idioms and epicenters of impact around the world. Thus he, and Neill after him, still beg the question about the significance of Christianity's new geographical center or centers and the forms of its new cultural identity or identities, about what Latourette calls Christianity's "geographic extent and potency." Thus the significance of Neill's question and Latourette's assertions lies in what they do not state rather than in what they do. Consequently, the question presses us to move beyond Christianity as "a universal religion," in Neill's language, to Christianity in its local expressions, in the forms in which the people of the world have clothed the religion as recognizably their own. As anyone will know from Neill's uncompromising account of the subject, he failed where Christianity succeeded. Neill failed because he remained still firmly fixed within the orbit and cultural center of the West, with the result that his book retains a distinctly European metropolitan outlook. For Neill, and others like him, the story of Christianity is the story of European missionaries and their doings and heroism among the natives. The epochal change that Neill claimed for Christianity as a religion that had shed, or was shedding, its European character, was scarcely reflected in the approach he adopted, and so we are left with a major hiatus between Christianity's genuinely worldwide character and Neill's own Eurocentric viewpoint. He took little account of the great movements of decolonization, of the new transformations and imperatives of nationalism in the *Tiers Monde,* or even, nearer home, of the movements for civil rights and racial justice. No wonder C. Vann Woodward, America's eminent historian of race relations, protested against white historiography on non-white peoples. Blacks, he said, have understandable causes for dissatisfaction with the academic status quo.

> For however sympathetic they may be, white historians with few exceptions are primarily concerned with the moral, social, political, and economic problems of white men and their past. They are prone to present to the Negro as *his* history the record of what the white man believed, thought, legislated, did and did not do *about* the Negro. The Negro is a passive element, the man to whom things happen. He is the object rather than the subject of this kind of history.... "The Negro Image" means the image in white minds. (1989: 35)

The old historiography had its centering in this kind of image-making. Yet, as John Peel pointed out in regard to social anthropology, nationalist movements in Asia and Africa threatened the old academic canons "with complete marginalization" if they "continued to ignore local intellectual agendas" (Peel, 1995: 581). Peel goes on to argue that Christianity in its missionary and localized forms offers social anthropologists and others an opportunity to deal with the credibility crisis of their discipline.

I cannot emphasize enough the scale of the crisis we face in the standard historiography of mission and world Christianity. The old line that the missionary brings light and truth and faith and love and all the other virtues secures for itself a channel in Western depictions of the enterprise, in Western accounts of the idea of mission, its proper implementation abroad, and the reception of it at local hands. Thus Neill brings the gifts of eloquence and passion to the task, saying the missionary "is engaged the whole time in making history, divine history. Things are happening today," he claims, "which have never happened before. In the mysterious providence of God, peoples which have never heard the Word of God, and were therefore without hope and without God in the world, are today hearing and believing" (Neill, 1964b: 268). In this reasoning, the providence of God is not mysterious enough to confound the missionary and reveal any worthwhile truth and virtue in local cultures. That is why Neill makes such remorseful reading today.

It could, however, be said in mitigation of Neill, and, in a different way of Latourette, that at least they saw which way the wind was blowing even though they resisted being swept in the same direction. Yet it remains an astonishing fact that, given their gifts of intellect and sympathy, both Neill and Latourette should proceed to tell the story of Christianity as essentially a phase of Europe's worldwide ascendancy after they had noted the cultural shifts that in their view were constitutive of the religion itself. The significance, then, of the work of Neill and Latourette lies beyond their works themselves; it lies in the perpetuation of their historical method by subsequent writers. Thus, for example, did Max Warren, an otherwise perceptive and sensitive interpreter of things missionary and historical, conceive the entire missionary enterprise as Western in its design and thrust. So he spoke almost instinctively of "us" and "them," of the responsibility of the West toward Asia and Africa, of the unquestioned superior right of the West to interpret what was happening in Asian and African Christianity without reference to Asians and Africans. It would be grossly unfair to charge Warren with jingoism or malice, but his historical method is profoundly limited by its Eurocentrism. He seemed unable to throw himself into the nationalist ferment that was stirring the peoples of Asia and Africa toward a new destiny. So Warren wrote about how "the revolt against the contempt of the white world" could not be sincere because those who led the revolt found themselves "compelled to depend upon that white world for the economic wherewithal to meet even the most modest of their economic ambitions" (Warren, 1965: 165). As such, the nationalist resurgence in colonized societies was reduced to this ineffectual flailing against a dominant West. Yet Warren dug deeper, saying Asians and Africans caught in the fervor of the anticolonial struggle had failed to invoke the mercy of God, as the Psalmist counseled ("Have mercy upon us, O Lord, have mercy upon us, for we have had more than enough of contempt. Too long our soul has been sated with the scorn of those who are at ease, the contempt of the proud" [Ps. 123:3–4]) and had instead "taken things into their own hands" (ibid.: 164). Yet how else can we be immersed in history except by taking things into our own hands through commitment, engagement, and action? It is no less unconvincing to say that missionaries are properly immersed in history while Asians and Africans for their part should desist from taking things into their own hands. If Warren, who was otherwise so imbued with spiritual wisdom and historical acumen, should nevertheless be so massively hindered by the old historiography, it boggles the mind to think of what happened, and continues to happen, to those of lesser endowment. But, for reasons of discretion, I will refrain from naming names here.

The one important exception to the perpetuation of the old historiography has been liberation theology, whose exponents have insisted on repudiating Eurocentrism and adopting instead the people's view of history. However, the shortcoming of liberation theology has been its relative failure to produce a commensurate stream of innovative historical works, though often that has not been for lack of trying.

Consequently, William Temple's observation of world Christianity as a new fact of our time remained relatively under-exploited and generally unnoticed. I happen to believe that the two things go together: that a new historiography, guided by the principles of local agency and indigenous cultural appropriation, and the prominence of world Christianity accompany each other in mutual reinforcement. Yet the obstacles to producing such a new historiography are formidable, and none more obdurate than the reluctance of Western scholars to abandon the view of missionary domination and incompatibility with local cultures, so that Christian contact tends to be construed only as political imposition and cultural interference, never as genuine local appropriation or even transformation. Yet this conspiratorial view of Christianity limits it to a top-down view of history, to the view of the impregnable nature of Western priorities and the derivative character of local responses and reactions, as Warren implies. Thus, while it suggests commendable Western self-criticism, such denunciation of missions still retains the focus on the West through its defaulting missionaries rather than on local agents and local processes, with the result of so-called global Christian history being left with colonialism and the colonial aftermath as its only subject matter and context.

The Colonial Frame

This colonial context has framed much of the discussion on missions and the consequences of missionary evangelization. For example, the founding president of Kenya, Jomo Kenyatta, charged the missionaries with wrecking native customs and traditions and with a frontal assault on the people's self-image. He said the missionaries regarded the African

> as a clean slate on which anything could be written. He was supposed to take wholeheartedly all religious dogmas of the white man and keep them sacred and unchallenged, no matter how alien to the African mode of life. The Europeans based their assumption on the conviction that everything the African did or thought was evil. (Kenyatta, n.d. [1938]: 259–60)

Africans were to be rescued from eternal fire, Kenyatta continues, and so the missionaries

> set out to uproot the African, body and soul, from his old customs and beliefs, and put him in a class by himself, with all his tribal customs shattered and his institutions trampled upon. The African, having been detached from his family and tribe, was expected to follow the white man's religion without questioning whether it was suited for his condition of life or not. (Ibid.)

A cardinal error of the West, according to Kenyatta, was to impose on Africans the West's individualism that wrought havoc on the people. Missionaries compounded the nature of foreign domination by sharpening the lines of attack and occupation that the colonialists had organized and extended on the military and political front.

An obvious response to Kenyatta's strictures is to say that missionaries did not succeed with him and the vast cohorts of Africans who filled the ranks of anti-missionary and anti-colonial agitation, that his own lucidness was proof that natives could outwit their missionary detractors and their colonial oppressors. Thus Kenyatta's criticisms muddy the waters of the Western encounter with non-Western peoples, because the language of national reaction was itself a fruit of that encounter. As such, Gikuyu mother tongue literacy, strengthened by the translated Gikuyu Bible, equipped Kenyatta and his compatriots with the discourse of self-rule and intellectual autonomy. At that point the effect of missions takes on radical local dimensions, prompting the question as to which of the three phases of the West's encounter with the non-Western world had the most significant long-term impact: (a) the project of colonial over-rule, (b) the creation of satellite mission communities insulated from African life, or (c) the introduction and practice of Christianity in its mother tongue version? The answer is clear. The first two phases contained the seeds of their own destruction, whereas the third phase struck deep roots in the culture, roots that outlived the ephemeral nature of alien rule and of marginal mission enclaves. Thus Kenyatta claims the Gikuyu Bible, the *Ibuka ria Ngai,* as a primer in nationalism, an approach that tacitly promotes Christianity as an ally of oppressed people and their downtrodden culture. So we may argue that Kenyatta's work as a nationalist political leader makes sense only in the context of indigenous initiatives that missionaries had taken, though for reasons very different from his own. As the unacknowledged child of Christian missions, therefore, Kenyatta and his political career demonstrate that there is more than a circumstantial coincidence between colonialism's long-term interests and the effects of mother tongue literacy pioneered by missions — that there is, in fact, a logical conflict.

Another approach to Kenyatta is to question his claims — to ask, for example, whether the historical evidence supports his contention that missionaries to a person failed to identify with Africans in their opposition to colonialism. Here the record is a great deal more complicated than Kenyatta contends. The Church Missionary Society missionary, Ludwig Krapf, and the Universities Mission to Central Africa missionary, Edward Steere, both of East Africa (Njogu, 1992: 69–76); Moffat and Livingstone of central and southern Africa; and Koelle, Zahn, and Zimmermann of West Africa, to take a random list, all show considerable flair and support for local language development and for the importance of mother tongue literacy. Krapf, for one, was in no doubt that European colonial rule would constitute a major long-term obstacle for Christianity, whatever the immediate appeal of colonial conquest (Krapf, 1860: 416–17). Robert de Nobili of India, Francis Xavier, Alessandro Valignano of Japan, and Matteo Ricci of China repeat this theme of indigenous cultural development for the Catholic tradition in the early modern period. Sometimes the effects on the missionaries of such long-term involvement with local cultures and traditions can be quite unexpected in terms of going native oneself. Robert de Nobili and Matteo Ricci, for example, demonstrate that fact in the Catholic missionary tradition, while a similar thing has been observed of Presbyterian missionaries in China (see Xi, 1997).

The development of a new historiography to reflect such indigenous priorities in mission and their further elaboration in world Christianity has been generally slow in emerging, though secular historians have shown greater willingness than their religious counterparts (e.g., Porter, 1997).

Compared to such secular interest, it is a curious thing that Western academic theologians (alas!) have scarcely shown any sustained interest in the subject, having decided to turn their backs on world Christianity as the offspring of mission's outdated theology of territorial expansionism. Academic theology is thus inclined to resolve issues of historical fact with contentions about human motives, with world Christianity inviting its appropriate quota of misgivings about local inadequacies and misunderstandings. However the missionaries may have represented Christianity, goes the theological argument, aboriginal populations could form no adequate concept of Christian doctrine to have embraced the religion correctly. So their profession of Christianity is misguided and mistaken, if not downright corrupted.

Try as you may to overcome such ideas of missionary hegemony and theological inadequacy, and you will find in the idiom of hegemony and victimization little room for maneuver. Yet the fact is that the unassailable nature of Western political ascendancy stands in contradiction to Western religious inadequacy, which in turn stands in conflict with the pernicious influence of missionary evangelization. You only worry about missionary evangelization if it seems able to win the natives — though if missionaries suffered from religious inadequacy, their evangelization should show it. The contradiction persists because the two parts of ascendancy and inadequacy do not add up.

Adjusting the Curriculum

Traditionally we tried to add up the historical gains of Christianity with the help of the tools of church history, although in so doing we did not notice the cross-cultural aspects of Christian history. Church history in its hallowed place in the theological curriculum plunges us into the deep end of classical Christian thought, too much so to be serviceable as we try to follow the tide of Christianity's global growth, expansion, and intercontinental connections. Church history is too closely tied to the old historiography, too deeply embedded in a top-down view of God in history, to take in the landscape of an emergent world Christianity with its roots among workers, peasants, refugees, immigrants, and the rural underclass.

One of the striking changes in our time is Christian identity taking on increasingly non-Western forms, becoming part and parcel of the religious history of once exotic and alien societies but ones that are now no longer remote. This modern-day indigenous formative process has caused Christianity effectively to shed its Western territorial complex and to become a new ecumenical and global force. Consequently, its history, traditionally reconstructed from literary and documentary sources housed in library and archival centers in the West and elsewhere, is now being reconstituted with those materials as well as with oral and eyewitness accounts based on non-Western experience. It happens that Yale University, for example, houses one of the most significant collections on world Christianity and has continued to devote considerable resources and expertise to the task. Similar research centers have grown up both here in the United States and elsewhere, and scholars and researchers nourished from these resources are increasingly willing to uncouple Christianity from its European political carriage and to see it as more than the unsavory tail-end of Western missions, more than a mummified specimen of Western colonial hegemony whose exotic Third World tribal survivals we may corral into an area studies specialty. In truth, world Christianity has become global in its range and multicultural in its impact; it represents an opportunity to expand religious history in a cross-cultural and comparative direction.

The academic study of the subject in that form requires a fresh conceptualization of the field, a conscious loosening of old constraints, the abandonment of self-imposed barriers, adjustments in curricular priorities, and redeployment of existing resources and structures, as well as interdisciplinary collaboration among relevant parts of the academy. It would also necessitate the long overdue intramural use of the important collections housed in research centers as well as in church and missionary collections.

It would, similarly, draw on untapped resources and expertise in secular departments of major research universities. The global and intercultural character of world Christianity demands expertise in numerous fields of academic specialization: history and religion are two obvious areas, but also anthropology, philosophy, human rights, politics, international relations, the study of language and literature, customary law, and indigenous healing systems.

History, Religion, and the Social Sciences

All of that suggests the value and imperative of collaborative multi-disciplinary work. It also suggests expanding the terms of historical knowledge. Both Latourette and Neill, for example, reflected little of the advances the social sciences had made into the domain historical knowledge has traditionally claimed for itself. The social sciences had benefited from what has been called "the epistemological liberalization" that stemmed from the impact of Locke and Newton and expanded with the new positivism promoted by Hume, Comte, Spencer, and others. Given the insistence of the social sciences that laws are to be understood as social rules, valid because they are enacted by the "sovereign" or derive logically from existing decisions, and that ideal or moral considerations should not limit the scope or operation of the law, it is perhaps understandable that Latourette and Neill, among others, ignored the otherwise pervasive influence of the social sciences. Social sciences' operative premise that knowledge exists in a watertight container that leaves no room for religion to slip in sounds off-putting to begin with. Perhaps Latourette and Neill were justified in their attitude. The hardcore, watertight claims of the social sciences themselves rest on the presupposition that society is like a biological organism, with conduct, behavior, and action rooted in sensation and reflection, and as such precluding considerations based on morality or intentionality. Were social scientists to leave room for religion, they would breach the walls of autonomy and objectivity they had erected for their subject.

Yet we cannot today ignore the social sciences even though we must resist history being turned into a doubt-free, cause-and-effect science, into a mechanical system of explanation and proof. Similarly, history cannot be made captive to the relentless repetitiveness of the chronicle, with its mechanistic rehearsal of facts. Thus, for example, did the classical Muslim historian, Bayhaqi, declaim such a mechanistic approach to history, saying:

> These stories may be far from history, where one usually reads that such and such a king sent such and such a general to such and such a war, and that on such and such a day they made war or peace, and that this one defeated that one, or that one this one, and then proceeded somewhere. But I write what is worthy to be recorded. (Cited in Lewis, vol. 2, 1987: frontispiece)

Sir Isaiah Berlin also rejects this mechanistic view of history, saying, "except on the assumption that history must deal with human beings purely as material objects in space — must, in short be behaviorist — its methods can scarcely be assimilated to the standards of an exact natural science" (Berlin, 1954: 52). Berlin returns to the issue elsewhere when he says a person "who lacks common intelligence can be a physicist of genius, but not even a mediocre historian" (Berlin, 1960: 30; see also Flew, 1958: 283–84). Beattie, a leading social anthropologist, agrees with this distinction with the natural sciences. "The crux of the matter," he explains, "is that for the most part the behavior of people in societies only makes sense when we seek to discover what they *think* they are doing, a mode of inquiry which would obviously be inappropriate if we are dealing, as 'natural' scientists, with (say) molecules or, for that matter, with the social life of white ants or bumble-bees" (Beattie, 1984: 5; see also Gellner, 1973).

The threefold character of social scientific inquiry, namely, its concern with what people do, what they think they are doing, and for what purpose, overlaps considerably with the method of social and intellectual history. Furthermore, the theological method, in terms of discourse about God, need not be in conflict with the methods of social and historical inquiry. Locke, for example, placed knowledge of God in the category of knowledge of real existence, and he distinguished that from knowledge about identity or diversity, knowledge about relation, and knowledge about co-existence or necessary connection. What values we assign to these different forms of knowledge depends on our starting point, depends on our premise, a premise that is not itself subject to scrutiny. Thus for Locke, intuitive or even probable knowledge is the first and most certain degree of knowledge: it is immediate, experience-based, and self-authenticating, rather than something innate in the mind. Yet the fact that I know intuitively that "red" and "white" do not represent the same idea does not say anything about how, under certain circumstances, knowledge of God may make a prior claim on my life or even how intuitive knowledge may, by a hunch, nudge me unbidden into transcendent mystery. Similarly, knowledge of co-existence or necessary connection, that is to say, knowledge of the scientific kind, demands that we bring future expectations to bear on physical and sense data, so that we may deepen logical extrapolation with normative reflection. Thus, to make room for knowledge in the religious sense, we need to make room in knowledge as a bio-psychological function, as a self-reinforcing process, for knowledge as an act of self-transcendence, as a facet of critical historical consciousness. Locke's legacy to the social sciences was the encouragement his ideas gave to "the development of a relative plurality of cognitive strategies to enrich the repertoire of rationalist, purely empiricist, and philosophically necessary causal explanatory strategies" (Olson, 1993: 90; see also Bidney, 1953; and Brown, 1984).

The historical discipline in our branch of study, and theology broadly construed, would be concerned significantly, though by no means exclusively, with the facts, effects, and consequences of the knowledge of God, both with its familiar expressions in the originating culture, and with its unfamiliar repercussions in its missionary field dimension. To do that well, we would need "a relative plurality of cognitive strategies," certainly, but also a plurality of idioms, contexts, and centers of gravity that would move us beyond merely causal explanatory strategies and beyond current shibboleths. I think the old historiography erred and undersold the subject by focusing almost entirely on the originating impulses of missions and world Christianity, and overlooking the vast terrain of the local effects and feedback. Yet, by the same token, I think the old historiography was instinctively right to reject a mechanistic view of history. Still, my regret remains that the old historiography did not appreciate that, because evidence is so fundamental to the nature and character of history, especially of religious history, it makes all the difference whether we include or exclude evidence derived from the social and field dimensions of Christian practice and teaching. The opportunity thus to present the history of Christianity from the bottom up, from the underside of society, so to speak, rather than from the top down and its support of institutional and structural privilege — this opportunity, I mean to say — was lost.

Defining the Shift

As we can see from all the preceding account, the change in world Christianity involves much more than demographic significance. It would be utterly remiss in a paper of this nature not to call attention to someone like Samuel Ajayi Crowther (1806–91), the first African bishop and the pioneer of Christianity in his native Nigeria. Crowther's career coincided with the formative Niger Mission (1841–91) in Nigeria which he headed, assisted by fellow Africans. Crowther's leadership was momentous for African Christianity: his translation of the Yoruba Bible was the first translation into an African language. In addition to Yoruba, Crowther wrote in the Igbo, Hausa, and Nupe languages. On his visit to London in 1851 at the instigation of Henry Venn, Crowther had interviews with Queen Victoria and Prince Albert, and such was the effect of his meetings that he was able to move a reluctant British government to intervene in Nigeria against the continuing slave trade.

Crowther's linguistic work was part of a larger theme of the missionary development of African languages, including the creation of vernacular alphabets, dictionaries, grammars, and lexicographies. The effects on the affected cultures of such linguistic work cannot be exaggerated. The grammars and dictionaries, for example, sparked wide-ranging cultural and social movements, thus encouraging local populations, Christian and non-Christian alike, to become authoritative exponents of their own history. Missionary translation work offered people a unique opportunity to grasp the native point of view, as the English missionary Bishop John Colenso of Durban, South Africa, astutely put it. Or as another missionary linguist, Christaller of Ghana, affirmed (1879), language contains the sparks of truth with which a culture accedes to its true potential, and no barrier of taboo, stigma, or unfamiliarity should be allowed to stand in the way. Diedrich Westermann, the German missionary linguist, summed up the case when he said that the vernacular is not the gift of the white man to the African but God's gift, and is as such the vessel in which is contained the whole national life and through which it finds expression (1925). One English missionary in South Africa challenged other missionaries to accept the only conclusion that is natural to draw from all the teeming linguistic and cultural evidence — namely, that "the law which holds the earth in its orbit and regulates the fall of a pin, is the same law which has directed the Greek to call God *theos* [and] has guided the Zulu to speak of Him as *Unkulunkulu*. And that law we must accept with its consequences" (Green, n.d.: 41). The successful development of African languages in Bible translation, in worship, prayer, and study, repeated the pattern first established at Pentecost where the assembled company could hear what was being said, "each one in his own language. And they were amazed and wondered, saying, 'Are not all these who are speaking Galileans? And how is it that we hear, each of us in his own native language? . . . we hear them telling in our own tongues the mighty works of God'" (Acts 2:6–8, 11). Thus destigmatized, the Gentiles, and their languages along with them, were freed to be included in God's design for the salvation of the world.

The Niger Mission under Crowther carried this Gentile charge by redirecting the focus from European leadership, finance, and scholarship to African agency and local support. Africans not only planned, directed, and implemented missionary policy, but they also went on to observe, to research, to document, and to reflect in original ways on how to do mission in an African context, producing linguistic materials, ethnographic surveys, historical studies, and religious accounts. Europeans at the time found this African achievement difficult to accept or acknowledge, resulting in a perplexing silence in many standard Western works on the chief African architects. Yet the Niger Mission, and the native pastorate it produced in Sierra Leone and elsewhere, places us firmly on the path that Africans blazed in the anti-slavery movement in the eighteenth and nineteenth centuries.

Thus did Africans read in historical events very different lessons. In that respect, when Japan defeated Russia in the Russo-Japanese war of 1905, public opinion in West Africa hailed it as a judgment on the cult of imperial power and as a providential sign that God and time were on the side of the underdog. Finally, when world war broke out in 1914, the news was assimilated into the apocalyptic signs and wonders of Prophet William Wadé Harris (1860–1929) of the Ivory Coast and Prophet Garrick Braide (1882–1918) of the Niger Delta in Nigeria, whose overlapping charismatic careers fanned the flames of popular social unrest and directed them into explicitly religious channels. In this way, Christianity and political developments combined to inspire Africa's critical awareness of its place in salvation history.

Two final themes must conclude our study. One is the effect of Vatican Council II (1963–65) on missions in Africa. Two particular documents of the Council are relevant, one being on missionary activity, *Ad Gentes,* which addressed mission as a special activity of the church rather than subsuming it under an all-purpose church function. "Mission is constitutive of the church," *Ad Gentes* stated, based in a trinitarian affirmation, with the bishops taking joint responsibility for it. The second document, *Lumen Gentium,* followed up the ideas of *Ad Gentes* with a discussion about mission bearing fruit in the establishment of local churches that in turn assume responsibility for further mission.

The convening of the African Synod, first at Rome in May 1994, and finally at Yaoundé, Cameroon, in September 1995, a milestone in the evolution of mission and Christianity in Africa, was a major step in taking up the statements of Vatican II and refocusing them on Africa. The African Synod was convened under the apostolic leadership of Pope John Paul II, who traveled to Cameroon in September 1995 to preside over its substantive deliberations. The Synod's detailed and extensive pronouncements, contained in the *Propositions* and introduced with a list of protocols describing the nature, scope, tasks, hopes, goals, and future direction of the work, marked a decisive step in the church's understanding of mission in Africa. The Synod in effect conceived the church as a radical, indigenously led missionary movement, committed to engagement with Africa's critical development priorities. For that purpose, the

Synod placed special emphasis on the continent's immense human potential and what that can contribute to global solidarity for peace, justice, and opportunity. If Vatican II was in part an attempt by the church to come to terms with the modern world, as one of its documents states, then another equally important dimension was its coming to terms with the implications of the missionary success of the church. That required the younger churches of Asia and Africa not to be absorbed into preexisting European structures and ideas. The church must reinvent itself to respond to changes in the former mission fields. The vernacular Mass that Vatican II had instituted opened the way for the kind of fundamental rethinking required, but it took the African Synod to draw out in a timely, concrete way the new paths to be followed in Africa.

The second of our final themes concerns what might be called the signature tune of African Christianity, namely, the rise and proliferation of African Independent churches led by charismatic religious figures noted for their appeal to dreams, prayer, and healing. Both Harris and Braide were such indigenous religious pioneers. Independency, as the phenomenon is known, was the African response to Christianity, first, to its excessive European political and cultural baggage, and, second, to its creative transformation in the African crucible. In its political temper, Independency splintered off into varieties of "Ethiopianism," that is, into forms of protest and resistance defined by racial and political concerns. In its essentially religious temper, however, Independency assumed the tones and color of Zionism, that is, charismatic and revivalist expressions that show considerable continuity and overlap with African religions. This process radically transformed Christianity into an Africanized religion. Here, too, we see Christianity profiting from positive as well as negative circumstances, with colonial repression, on the one hand, exciting millenarian Ethiopianism and political independence, on the other hand, removing the brakes on spontaneous indigenous development, as the charismatic renewal and expansion prove. It was a process that would produce world Christianity and a new anthropology, that is, Christianity as a truly world religion increasingly defined by the values and idioms of non-Western cultures, languages, and concepts.

Concluding Observations

Mary Kingsley (1899) once observed that the progress of Christianity in Africa was *Bon-gré, mal-gré,* bound up with the vital influence that African traditional religions, what she called "Fetish," intending no pejorative stigma, were able to impart, "a sea wherein all things suffer a sea change." Her acute prediction has been borne out by events since then. In medieval Europe, all a Christian ruler had to do to convert his subjects was to force the religion on them and, with little or no knowledge of the religion, have them baptized en masse. In modern Africa, by contrast, that medieval solution to the problem of Christianity failed completely, and chiefs themselves led the opposition to missions. Rather, Christianity put down roots from means more conciliatory and agreeable. Thus did Christian Independency, for example, use dreams, prayer, prophecy, and healing to institute reforms in music, regalia, liturgy, and pastoral counseling, and so to minister to their throngs of converts. True, some of the innovations, not yet matured by precedent and inflamed by official intransigence, veered toward the eclectic and naive, though the example, being at once patriotic and novel, attracted the attention of mainline churches which responded with their own thoughtful variations on the theme. The result is that Africa's Christian population has exploded to over three hundred million, with the continent being shaped as a new Christian heartland. The numerical scale of growth is matched only by the paradigm shift of acute indigenous inculturation. That African shift, consequently, is more than chronological, involving, as it does, a radical change of perspective from Christianity as inescapable. Spiritual opportunity, not political stratagem, would define the religion's identity for its new adherents.

Thus is apostolic Christianity now set, after having been a medieval state orthodoxy and after becoming a sub-plot of European maritime expansion that fueled slavery and colonialism, to divest itself of its Western cultural and political baggage and ready to be drilled by culturally charged forces into its Gentile African pivot. This convergence between Christianity and the lively historical pagan heritage would accrue credit to Christianity — as Aquinas said of the pagan heritage of the early church fathers.

The decisive identity question for Christian Africa, then, turns on the nature of the transition from a territorial, scholastic church of the medieval period to evangelical, disestablishmentarian forms of the religion; from the concordat approach to mission to Independency and personal lay agency; and from metropolitan *assimilados* to vernacular translation and rural empowerment. What subsequently distinguished African Christianity was its being invested with the idiom of mother tongue translation and its emerging from its indigenous transformation as a mass movement, fluent in the native Scriptures, untrammeled by Western borrowings, and able to respond to local life and values with inborn confidence.

In our day, we could say that a millennium of Christian history has come to an end, and the characteristics by which the religion has customarily been identified are no longer with us. If for centuries Christian expression has been shaped and tested by the environment of the Mediterranean world and of the lands to the north and west of it, today the religion is being reformulated in the diverse conditions of Africa, China, Japan, Melanesia, India, and Latin America — regions with their own priorities, flavor, and style. The effect on Christianity is unmistakable. What historians once described as the "acute Hellenization" of Christianity in the change from Jerusalem to Antioch and Athens, we may describe today as the "acute indigenization" of the faith that has led to changes in Christian priorities and in the structure of Christian thought, government, and practice. Much of this has come about only since the 1950s; that is, in the period since political independence (Walls, 1987: 80–81).

As a concomitant of these changes, Christianity can no longer be conceived exclusively in denominational terms along the threefold division of Orthodox, Catholic, and Protestant. A new historical method is required to deal with emerging forms of the religion in lands lying beyond the West. In the light of the new reality, such a denominational division makes less sense even though the structures sustaining old mental habits are slow to respond to the change. It is generally accepted today that any important theological contribution should have an influence far beyond one denomination; the insights and discoveries of each ecclesial tradition should find reciprocity and acceptance in the others (ibid.: 87).

The modern missionary movement had a lot to do with this emerging ecumenical consciousness, though few at the time could have foreseen that. This was true especially for theologians, as Andrew Walls has pointed out in remarking on the slowness of Western academic theology to respond to developments in world Christianity, a surprising fact because in the nineteenth century theology had responded with energy and deepening insight to the changes afoot in several branches of learning — in archeology, in the discovery of papyri and the text criticism it fostered, in the historical sciences and in the natural sciences, and in changes in society.

> While all this was happening, a still greater fund of new discoveries was coming to light in Asia and Africa, with the capacity for a still greater impact on the Christian mind; but its importance for theology was not immediately recognized. It was secular learning that first felt the impact

of the missionary encounter with Africa and Asia. Missionary scholarship established new boundaries; it established whole new disciplines (African linguistics is a direct fruit of mission activity) and revolutionized others. Scientific anthropology was made possible by the missionary movement; it was not something the early missionaries simply omitted to take with them. The same is true of the comparative study of religion and the phenomenology of religion that is its product. For a long time there was little understanding of other cultures. When Robert Morrison was appointed a missionary to China in 1807, the entire Chinese resources of British academic libraries consisted of one manuscript in the British Museum and one in the Royal Society, and not a person in Britain read or spoke Chinese. When Morrison returned on his first and only furlough (now the translator of the Bible and author of a massive Chinese dictionary), he took steps to establish an Oriental philological institute. Missionaries such as James Legge, the greatest English-speaking sinologist of the nineteenth century, and J. N. Farquhar, who did so much to interpret Indian literature in the twentieth, helped to open up the West to classical religious, philosophical, and historical texts of Asia. But no one, not even missionaries for the most part, realized the theological implications of all this learning. Theology was still a *datum.* Today, with a new phase of Christian history well launched in the lands that gave rise to this new knowledge, we have a theological El Dorado wholly comparable with the rich discoveries and new science of a century ago. It has fallen to those of us in mission studies to have our humble daily labor in the very territory that includes the path to El Dorado. (Walls, 1991: 149)

New discoveries take time to sink in and to overturn accepted standards. The discovery of the New World, for example, was not immediately reflected in European cartography, let alone allowed to replace the old maps and the intellectual assumptions they enshrined.

In fact, the new discoveries were intellectually threatening, requiring the abandonment of too many certainties, the acquisition of too many new ideas and skills, the modification of too many maxims, the sudden irrelevance of too many accepted authorities. It was easier to ignore them and carry on with the old intellectual maps (and often the old geographical maps too), even while accepting the fact of the discovery and profiting from the economic effects. (Ibid.: 150)

Yet those of us who stand today with a breathtaking view of the headwaters of the new world Christian movement must demand fresh navigational aids. We must simply reject old assurances; reject attempts at projecting the old ideas of organization, control, and direction into the future; and instead ask new questions without reference to the old answers. We should demand that mission and world Christianity be thematized with reference to the forms, symbols, liturgies, and prayers of the people represented.

When Acton said that history was not a web woven by innocent hands, he might as well have been referring to the contentious legacy of the modern missionary movement. His words also remind us of the status in that movement of the colonized, whose voice has been effectively silenced in the retelling of the missionary story. Both Neill and Warren, for example, achieve this silencing of the colonized voice, perhaps because the rapid pace of decolonization had caught Neill and Warren unawares and left them with nowhere else to put the new wine of nationalism except in the old wineskins of European imperial ascendancy. Yet, who dares to fault them, except that they undersell the subject and belittle the significance of what missionaries accomplished, however unwittingly.

Anyone concerned with the merits of the issue will want to retrieve the history of missions and world Christianity from its captivity in colonial studies and to place it squarely where it belongs: within the unfolding narrative of humanity's struggle for freedom, justice, and equality.

There are today extraordinary currents stirring in our midst, and world Christianity belongs to that general process. We find, for example, fresh energy and intelligence are being devoted to the production of new hymns, music, and artistic and liturgical materials; to the creation of fresh categories for doing theology; to the retrieval of threatened cultural resources; to the application of religion to public agenda issues; and to the promotion of ecumenical sharing and partnership. By virtue of such efforts, new identities are being forged, new boundaries established for freedom and justice, and new loyalties promoted to remove ancient suspicions and antagonisms. All these variegated activities are shaped and expressed through oral and written narratives and through the experiences and expectations that in turn shape and direct the narratives. It is this multi-layered fact that makes the Christian narrative so complex and so resistant to mechanistic explanation, for, as John Peel observed with regard to anthropology,

> narratives-as-lived are the proper subject matter of an historical anthropology and that any anthropology that takes seriously the idea of

human agency will be concerned with how narratives-as-lived are shaped
by narratives-as-told.... Here, the narratives-as-told are not only those
that individuals tell of their own and their relatives' and acquaintances'
recent pasts, but the canonical (and in a way collective) stories contained
in Scripture and the consolidated oral tradition of their communities.
(Peel, 1995: 606–7)

All such activity constitutes a public imperative for change. It may be easier
for us to carry on with the old approaches, more comfortable to draw on
the old intellectual capital, and more reassuring to rely on the old unilateral
reserves of Western power, but it is patently no longer adequate to the new
developments and challenges of the field. We are witnessing today a crucial
shift from Christianity's external relations, from its missionary burden and
controversy, to matters pertinent to local potential and experience. There has
been a landslide change in the old order, an axial shift of mass and direction.
We need new tools and structures and altogether a new attitude toward the
dynamic and plural nature of world Christianity. It is the only way to save and
serve the cause.

— S I X —

THE ONGOING TASK

Agenda for a Work in Progress

*Mark Hutchinson (chair), Pablo Deiros, Klaus Korschorke,
Donald Lewis, Melba Maggay*

The term "global" immediately questions the edges of traditional history that from its (modernist) golden age in the nineteenth century has been located on the national stage. Challenged by the pluralism and "other centeredness" of postmodernizing culture, the central tenets of such modernist nation-making history have been widely challenged, though, as some of the contributors to this volume suggest, the challenge has been longer coming in certain areas of history than in others. The revisionism that has crept into the discipline has tended to go two ways: either through world systems theory toward universal and comparative history, or through gender, ethnic, or political foci toward "bottom up" studies locally or regionally situated. This trend has been driven by waves of theory, including new societies theory, frontier theory, gender theory, and the crossover effects of developments in literary theory and social theory. In neither direction — outward toward comparative history or inward to local history — have the challenges of globalization theory, questioning such quanta as time and space, and requiring the description of "glocalities" really been tackled.

Likewise, the challenges implicit in the term "Christian historiography" — a phrase that immediately places faith and discipline in tension — have not been unpacked. The master in the field, Herbert Butterfield, grappled with the questions of faith in the context of international history and "scientific history" rather than in the dystopian context of the postmodern world. Consequently, Butterfield's work leaves much to be done in the overlapping fields covered by this volume.

The historiographical task ahead of us can be visualized in terms of four categories: (a) epistemology, or ways of knowing in Christian history; (b) research methodology of historiographical enterprise; (c) new definitions; and (d) agenda for accomplishing the task.

Epistemological Challenges and Responses

One of the key problems associated with a project to reorient Christian historiography is to move forward rather than relapsing into Babel. The methodological problem is considerable. Many historians have enough trouble finding the time and research resources to finish many *local* projects. To take on a vast global enterprise is a daunting prospect indeed. This hesitation is reinforced by a strong suspicion bred into us by the way we have traditionally learned church history via texts like Latourette (1953), Walker (1985), etc. According to the standard account, the Christian testimony moved from Jerusalem to Rome, then to England and Northern Europe; and then, after several centuries, to the United States and eventually through the missionary movement in English to the rest of the world. It presumes the Europeanization and, more recently, the Americanization of cultures that local historians, in their sympathy for the subjects, resist mightily. And so they should. Reinforcement of such homogenization cannot be the aim of a new historical paradigm if the aim is that of keener understanding.

The epistemological problem mentioned above, however, suggests that all resistance to the global ideal is not simply based on historical sympathy. It also stems from the fact that our imaginations fail to encompass the breadth of the subject. We do not easily think globally; our natural human reflex is to write within the comfortable national boundaries that have shaped the paradigm for historiography — which after all arose as partner to the nation-making process in early modern times and determined the burying places of the ancestors. Even the paradigm for cross-cultural work which has been dominant in many of our circles, and which has given rise to the institutional "ecumenism" of groups such as the World Council of Churches and the Lausanne movement, does not have within it the fullness of the biblical concept of *oikumene*. It remains tied to the concept of international cooperation of national representative bodies. How then do we begin to construct a global historiography?

The biblical response would seem to be that the choice is between Babel and the Body — the confusion of tongues, or the unity given us in the Body of Christ. We are impelled by the ideal of the Body to seek for more adequate ways of expressing the "fullness of Christ." In the words of Andrew Walls,

"Christ belonged to all humanity, and that the good news of Christ could be intelligibly received by all humanity" (Walls, 1996: xviii) has motivated the ceaseless effort to witness to the gospel in all cultures. Consequently, we have an imperative to be faithful not only to the global historiographical challenge but to the *Christian* historiographical challenge.

Traditionally, following the logic of Augustine of Hippo in his *City of God* and the even more inexorable logic of having to present the content of church history in a prescribed introduction to church history in theological colleges around the world, we have understood the "events" of church history sequentially. Such logic forces events into time frames that may or may not be justified by the events themselves. Alternatively, a biblical, multi-centered approach will lead to a more relational understanding of events. These may be evaluated in terms of how they represent God's redemptive actions in history. This requires a more organic model than is normal in most Western historiography, a model with Jesus Christ as the center of a relational process and network. We need to ask: "What was God doing here and here and here at the same time?" God was acting around the world through Christians and non-Christians alike. A true global history will pay attention to these factors.

In responding to the epistemological question, "What is a global historiography?" typically we start with a rather casual assumption that what we are talking about allows for easy exchanges between the terms "globe," "global," and "globalization." Similarly, "ecumenism" and *oikumene* at first sight appear to be equivalent. But as we engage in serious discussion and seek to clarify our conceptions of the world and of the globe, we soon discern that these terms are still being filtered through the preconceptions of nation-based histories. For those who come from countries with a long tradition of a state church, and with institutional ecumenism in place, the equivalence between ecumenism and *oikumene* is taken for granted. It is less obvious to those who came from countries with a stronger revivalist tradition or multi-national and multi-ecclesiastical experiences. Clearly, we cannot escape the task, identified by Andrew Walls in chapter 1, of reconceptualizing our view of the globe and to engage with the process of theorizing about globalization that is going on outside the walls of most theological institutions. To treat globalization as a replacement for the capitalist concepts of progress is to substitute once more a human nostrum for the providence of God, while to regard it as the great Satan is to misunderstand the nature of historical forces. As Lamin Sanneh noted, globalization is not a salvific process. It is simply the new context in which we seek to do justice and live the life of Christ.

Research Methodology

Our second question is: "What is the Christian approach to a global historiography?" Reflecting on the kind of historiography practiced by North American church historians at present, Henry Warner Bowden observed that the guild is still occupied with an insular view of history, one that focuses on the West in the narrow meaning of that term.[1] To move toward a global historiography we need new paradigms, but we will not get them by following the traditional paths. A point made repeatedly was that those who are searching for new paradigms must do so in isolation. Lacking precedents and colleagues who share their quest, these scholars are developing their methodologies through a process of trial and error and questioning of personal identity. Professor Mundadan reported that "his experience has confirmed his approach." In his moving statement, Professor Leung noted that in the face of the vastness of China, not to mention the globe, he proceeded by explicating his personal interaction with his subject field. Professor Pillay lifted the lid a little on his life in South Africa in an Indian community on the wrong side of the legal color bar of the white minority, and yet on the wrong side of the ethnic color bar of the black majority. Globalization radically questions personal identity, and each of these personal stories is a testimony to the situation in which both Christian people and Christian historians find themselves as cultural boundaries shift. Likewise, the "personal" emerged constantly in the professional fears that the local would get lost in the regional would get lost in the global. Such statements were not merely the expression of a fear about some paper product, but about the erasing of *place* before the bulldozers of American property developers, be that property physical, intellectual, emotional, or a figment held in memory and so crucial to personal and group identity.

There are many examples of the rather nasty reciprocal effects of globalization. Further, it is an overlooked corollary of Professor Mundadan's statement that decolonization is now almost complete. An urgent priority is to envision local histories that do not erase the local or the regional, but which emphasize glocality, the local presented against the background of the global. A further goal, as Phillip Leung reminds us, is to rise above the standard categories developed in the post-Bandung era to describe Western imperialism and to seek

---

1. Henry Warner Bowden. 1998. A Situation Report on North American Historiography in the Twentieth Century. Paper presented at Consultation Toward a Global Christian Historiography. Unpublished.

to describe what is happening in dynamic categories that take account of the Other. As he discovered, he was in fact becoming the Other.

A corollary of this is the question: At the start of the third millennium is there a new concept of how we actually write history? Are we using more ecumenical and global categories as the center moves toward the South and East? What is the relationship between the broader context and the specificity of national contexts? What happens when the edges shift if the center is defined by the edges? The answer we have already seen is that we lose identity. Globalization means we perceive something that has a horizon but no edges. Pentecostal churches in regions such as Latin America are growing not only among humble pagans who are passive receivers, but they are part of a process of cultural exchange. The result is that the very idea of the missionary-sending relationship has changed. Mission is taking place in a global perspective. Among many Pentecostals, for example, the South-South relationship is stronger than the North-South relationship. Ogbu Kalu has shown that missions are turning into NGOs (non-governmental organizations), rather than sending missions, per se, and networking has replaced independent action.[2] Instead of doing mission, we sponsor "projects." A sense of the global explains this change in relationship and methodology. In "projects" the edges are increasingly defined as being internal to the effort rather than being implicit in the group to whom the mission is directed.

In the new situation we have a multiplicity of centers, not just one. How then do we reorganize history? Following the example of Andrew Walls, we need to retrieve accounts of polycentricity in the past. This has direct implications, for example, for the writing of denominational histories where the power of the original North Atlantic center over the "edges" is rapidly fading. The decaying of peripheries is a major theme of our new history.

The old heartlands find it difficult to surrender ideas of periphery. This increases rather than decreases hostility as the old center refuses to recognize the emergence of new ones. As the uniqueness of the local is accentuated, we are driven toward the sort of history written by medieval historians — detailing the history of private and public, the effects that confessing Christianity has had on crucial elements such as the family and lifestyle across time in different cultures. If this is to be more than just another fad, we must ask Kalu's hard question: What is the purpose of this history and for whom am I writing? If

---

2. Ogbu Kalu. 1998. "Jesus Christ, Where Are You?" Themes in West African Church Historiography at the Edge of the Twenty-first Century. Paper presented at Consultation Toward a Global Christian Historiography. Unpublished.

we accept this model and apply this question, the result stretches beyond the production of text to the incarnation of the results. It becomes incumbent on Christian historians — as opposed to church historians, for instance, to help change the perceptions of Christians throughout the world with regard to the fact that the centers of Christianity have shifted from the North to the South and East. This has huge ramifications for such things as the "struggle for Christian America," which seems to have filled the bookshelves of that country several times over. The corollary to this is that if by struggling for "Christian America" — or Britain, or Germany, or whatever — is meant that America is a continuation of Christendom, it will never be found. It got up and moved south some years ago.

Redefinition

As suggested above, a number of methodological issues arise when we shift our attention from the periphery to the horizon, from the old centers, viewed seriatim, to a multi-centered world. This points to a series of new definitions.

1. *Christian history.* When we approach Christian history globally, an initial decision must be made: What is meant by Christian history? If the *history of Christianity* is intended, we must consider not merely the Christian community but the impact of Christianity on culture. No particular extra-professional requirements for action flow from this; one can approach the subject as a Christian or not. It is essentially religious history with Christianity as the subject. If the focus is on church history, in the sense of the institutional history of the church, again, I may adopt whatever categories may be applied to human institutions that fit the thesis. If I adopt the approach that my Christian history is the history of any selected field seen through Christian eyes, then theology, but not just theology, is required. The church becomes the subject, just as it could be Disneyland or cattle farming in Argentina. The inquiry is not a priori in predicting ends, but seeks knowledge, wisdom — in the biblical sense of the word — and life applications.

2. *The global.* A second initial choice relates to my attitude toward the globe. If I attempt to tackle the whole, it will crush me and no history will be written. If I ignore it, no global history can be written. But if I choose, as Gerald Pillay suggests, to use it as the background for my thought, then I can equally write about the said hypothetical Latin American *vacas*, and yet refer them to the international trade in beef, transportation routes, the impact of freezer technology, competition from lean-eyed Crocodile Dundees in Australia, and

the like. I can write my local church history and retain its locality. The difference is that I will write about that locality not as an existential thing in itself, an island in the stream of existence, but as a point through which various forces, people, and influences pass, and then emerge and reconnect to the global background. Locality does not disappear, individuality does not disappear, but locality and individuality are contextualized in the widest possible sense.

3. *Space and time.* In terms of end product, writing global history pushes us to privilege the elements of space and time. The first result is to anchor, as Professor Pillay has suggested, the historical boat in the long view. This allows providence to play a free role in any work's theological underpinnings. One must do more than this, however. "Time" must not be treated simply as chronology. Perceptions of time shift from one culture to another. As globalization theorist Roland Robertson has pointed out, globalization is the compression of time and space. The past to which we anchor ourselves is never static but flows away from us faster and faster as the pace of globalization accelerates.

The Christian historian is under mandate to remember the works of God, and so we need to reclaim those Christian gifts for modern historiography, teleology, and organic perception. Seeking to avoid disempowering local history by emphasizing cultural continuities as well as discontinuities, we point the hand of time forward as well as to the past. We reaffirm the nature of community by giving it an essential place in the world. Taking a global view need not destroy the faith community. It also must be noted that space and time are not the only horizons for the Christian historian. (a) We have the horizon of scripture, which provides edges for the sort of moral conundrums Kalu described (1998) based on African experience. (b) There are time horizons, such as Pillay hypothesizes with the onrushing of millennia. (c) There are spiritual horizons, as with the revivals of New England in 1730, Parramatta in 1830, and Tanzania in 1930, times when the spiritual reality overlays the globe so that it replaces other horizons. Christians are well equipped for this task.

We need not be trapped in the tendency of global histories to mandate space and time, for we have a long tradition of universal history — a perception of the great cloud of witnesses that look upon our efforts from the sidelines. Globalization relativizes the universal history of the church, because the compression of time and the rise of crises beyond the control of single nation-states mean that only the present is important and there is no ability to speak of transcendental realities. Part of the task of Christian history, therefore, is to hold the line, and not avoid the issue by ceding the hermeneutical task to the historical profession rather than the people of God.

4. *Inclusive history.* In terms of both method and content, this new history is inclusive. It describes the local by looking closely at the details; but then the local is held up against the horizon.

Agenda

To work at the historiographical task outlined above will require a range of new resources — conceptual and practical. This agenda lists a series of steps that ought to be taken in order to facilitate this work.

1. Develop cooperative histories between regions, comparing, say, Indonesia and Muslim states in West Africa; or, comparative histories looking at the parallels of, say, independent churches in Africa, India, and Australasia, all of which arise around the same time but which to this point have been explained by radically different means.

2. A register of sources on Asia, Africa, the Pacific, and Latin America in English (e.g., a Web-based database or on CD-ROM).

3. Facilitate collections of local histories in a coordinated manner so that their fields overlap and build over time toward regional libraries.

4. Intensify promotion of and new initiatives in such important bridging works as Donald Lewis, ed., *International Dictionary of Evangelical Biography,* and Scott Sunquist, ed., *Dictionary of Asian Christianity.* Based on his experience, Sunquist suggested the need to build up regional focus centers in places like Singapore, Bangalore, and Pretoria, etc., both to solve the serious problems of preserving source materials and for replicating the sorts of training programs for Christian historians that Trinity College (Singapore) has sponsored.

5. "Discipling" centers that can act to encourage younger historians to enter the field, already aware of the challenge of globally oriented scholarship. For example, most Australian history written by Christians has been shaped either by the paradigm of the secular university or that of the pulpit. One has to assume that most of these people will continue to be trained in the conventional ways, thus ensuring that Christian history will largely be driven by the requirements of particular social and historical entities. We must take steps to stretch the boundaries. This should be done in each of the regions as well as at major academic centers such

as Edinburgh, New Haven, London, and Kingston with rich library and archival resources as well as visionary mentors.

6. Development of studies that look at global experiences that are common across various localities and cultures. The new historiography needs to be multi-centered, just as is global Christianity. Examples of such studies include the localization of science and technology; the Bible as a common element in all Christian cultures; the idea of a common apostolic tradition; education and its interaction with localities; problems of postmodernity and how it interacts with Christianity; the problems of regional identity: how people perceive themselves and their perceptions of community. There are also important questions of terminology and categorization to be solved. What, after all, is Africa? What is the West? What is Asia? What does it mean to be "multi-centered"? And how have these concepts changed over time as conceptualization of the globe has changed?

7. In addition to the content of studies, modes of dissemination for new projects must be given due attention. Language is a real issue. For instance, there is a massive and growing literature on evangelicalism in Portuguese and Spanish that is generally inaccessible to monolingual English speakers. The "consciousness of place" element that flows from old Christendom ideas of South America as a Catholic domain, and modern American ideas of Latin America as its hegemonic backyard are subtexts that remain in the English world's conceptualization of history. Both linguistic and cultural issues have to be overcome in order to reinstate Latin America to its place in global Christian historiography.

8. Gender historians have long been working toward issues of the "other," of multi-centeredness, and of history from below. A global history has many lessons to learn and connections to make with the work of historians of gender.

9. The theme of "global historiography" is widely discussed today. Various initiatives are under way to reconceptualize historiography and sponsor projects in which new kinds of history can be undertaken. It is important to be aware of these programs and, where possible, collaborate.

References Cited

Agulhon, Maurice. 1982. *The Republic in the Village: The People of the Var from the French Revolution to the Second Republic.* New York: Cambridge University Press.

Baago, Kaj. 1969. *Pioneers of Indigenous Christianity.* Madras: CLS.

Barraclough, G. 1955. *History in a Changing World.* Oxford: Basil Blackwell.

———. 1967. *History and the Common Man.* London: The Historical Association.

Baur, F. C. 1968. *On the Writing of Church History.* Ed. and trans. P. C. Hodgson. New York: Oxford University Press.

Bays, Daniel H., ed. 1996. *Christianity in China: From the Eighteenth Century to the Present.* Stanford: Stanford University Press.

Beattie, J. H. M. 1984. "Objectivity and Social Anthropology." In S. C. Brown, ed., *Objectivity and Cultural Divergence.* Royal Institute of Philosophy Lecture Series, no. 17. Cambridge: Cambridge University Press, 5.

Berlin, Isaiah. 1954. *Historical Inevitability.* London: Oxford University Press.

———. 1960. "History and Theory." *Studies in the Philosophies of History* 1: 30.

Berry, Thomas. 1987. In Anne Lonergan and Caroline Richards, *Thomas Berry and the New Cosmology.* Mystic, Conn.: Twenty-Third Publications.

Bidney, David. 1953. "The Concept of Value in Modern Anthropology." In *Anthropology Today: An Encyclopedic Inventory.* Chicago: University of Chicago Press, 682–99.

Boff, Leonardo. 1991. *New Evangelization.* Maryknoll, N.Y.: Orbis Books.

Bowden, H. W. 1991. *Church History in an Age of Uncertainty.* Carbondale: Southern Illinois University Press.

———. 1998. "A Situation Report on North American Historiography in the Twentieth Century." Unpublished.

Broomhall, A. J. 1981–1989. *Hudson Taylor and China's Open Century.* 7 vols. London: Overseas Missionary Fellowship.

Brown, S. C., ed. 1984. *Objectivity and Cultural Divergence.* Royal Institute of Philosophy Lecture Series, no. 17. Cambridge: Cambridge University Press.

Bühlmann, Walbert, O.F.M. 1977. *The Coming of the Third Church: An Analysis of the Present and Future of the Church.* Maryknoll, N.Y.: Orbis Books.

Burke, Peter. 1991. *New Perspectives on Historical Writings.* Cambridge, U.K.: Polity Press.

Butterfield, H. 1965. *The Present State of Historical Scholarship: An Inaugural Lecture.* Cambridge: Cambridge University Press.

Carr, E. H. 1986. *What Is History?* Cambridge: Macmillan.

Cha Shih-chieh. 1983. *Zhongguo Jidujiao renwu xiaochuan* (Biographical Sketches on Chinese Christians). Vol. 1. Taipei: Zhonghua Fuyin shengxue yuan.

CHAI. 1974. "Scheme for a Comprehensive History of Christianity in India." *Indian Church History Review* 8: 89.

Christaller, Johannes G. 1989. *Twi Proverbs.* Basel: Evangelical Missionary Society.

Cohen, Paul A. 1963. *China and Christianity: The Missionary Movement and the Growth of Anti-foreignism, 1860–1870.* Cambridge, Mass.: Harvard University Press.

————. 1984. *Discovering History in China: American Historical Writings on the Chinese Recent Past.* New York: Columbia University Press.

Constable, Nicole. 1994. *Christian Souls and Chinese Spirits: A Hakka Community in Hong Kong.* Berkeley: University of California Press.

Correia-Afonso, John, S.J. 1969. *Jesuit Letters and Indian History, 1542–1773.* Bombay: Oxford University Press.

Cousins, Ewert H. 1979. "Raimundo Panikkar and the Christian Systematic Theology of the Future." *Cross Currents* 29: 142.

Croce, B. 1941. *History as the Story of Liberty.* London: George Allen & Unwin.

Daniels, David D. 1993. "Teaching History: U.S. Christianity in a Global Perspective." *Theological Education* 29 (spring): 91–111.

David, S. I. 1988. "Church History: History as Lived by Christian People." *The Asia Journal of Theology* 2: 106–8.

Despland, M. 1983. "How Close Are We to a Full History of Christianity? The Work of Jean Delumeau." *Religious Studies Review* 9 (January): 24–32.

Dussel, Enrique. 1985. "Towards a History of the Church in the World Periphery." In Lucas Vischer, ed., *Towards a History of Church in the Third World: The Issue of Periodization.* Bern: Evangelische Arbeitsstelle Oekumene Schweiz.

Eagleson, John, and Philip Scharper, eds. 1979. *Puebla and Beyond: Documentation and Commentary.* Maryknoll, N.Y.: Orbis Books.

EATWOT. 1997. "Final Statement of the Fourth General Assembly of EATWOT." *Vidyajyoti* 61: 247–57.

Elton, G. R. 1991. *Return to Essentials: Some Reflections on the Present State of Historical Study.* Cambridge: Cambridge University Press.

Evans, G. R. 1994. *The Church and the Churches.* Cambridge and New York: Cambridge University Press.

Fairbank, John K., ed. 1984. *The Missionary Enterprise in China and America.* Cambridge, Mass.: Harvard University Press.

Fears, J. Rufus, ed. 1988. *The Selected Writings of Lord Acton.* Vol. 3. *Essays in Religion, Politics, and Morality.* Indianapolis: Liberty Classics.

Ferro, M. 1984. *The Use and Abuse of History.* London: Routledge & Kegan Paul.

Flew, Anthony. 1958. Review of Popper's *The Poverty of Historicism, Sociological Review* 6, no. 2: 283–84.

Franzen, A. 1966. "Church History: Periodization." In Karl Rahner, ed. *Sacramentum Mundi.* New York: Herder and Herder, 1:366–73.

Gassmann, G. 1995. "The Global Context of Ecumenical History." In T. J. Wengert and C. B. Brockwell, Jr., eds. *Telling the Churches' Story: Ecumenical Perspectives on Writing Christian History.* Grand Rapids, Mich.: Eerdmans, 37–52.

Geddes, Michael. 1694. *The History of the Church of Malabar from the Time of Its First Being Discovered by the Portuguezes in the Year 1501: Giving an Account of the Persecutions and the Violent Method of the Roman Prelates to Reduce Them to the Church of Rome.* With the Synod of Diamper. London: Sam Smith and Benj Welford.

Gellner, Ernest. 1973. *Cause and Meaning in the Social Sciences.* London: Routledge.

Gender and History 1, no. 1 (spring 1989).

Gonzalez, J. L. 1993. "Globalization in the Teaching of Church History." *Theological Education* 29 (spring): 49–71.

Goodall, Norman. 1954. *A History of the London Missionary Society, 1895–1945.* London: Oxford University Press.

de Gouvea, Antonio. 1606. OESA, *Jornada do Arcebispo de Goa Dom Frey Aleixo de Menezes.* Published together with the Decrees of Synod of Diamper. Coimbra: Officina de Diogo Gomez Loureyro.

Green, James. "An Inquiry into the Principles Which Should Regulate the Selection of a Word to Denote 'God' in the Language of a Heathen Race: With Special Application to the Case of the Zulus." N.p., n.d.

Greinacher, Norbert. 1994. "Catholic Identity in the Third Epoch of Church History." *Concilium,* no. 5: 3–14.

Gurevich, Aron Iakovlevich. 1988. *Medieval Popular Culture: Problems of Belief and Perception.* New York: Cambridge University Press.

Habib, Irfan, K. N. Panikkar, and Romila Thapar. 1997. *Frontline.* Independence Jubilee Special (August 14): 55–63.

Hewitt, Gordon. 1971 and 1977. *The Problems of Success. A History of the Church Missionary Society, 1910–1943.* 2 vols. London: SCM Press.

The Hindu. International Edition. 1998. March 28: 14.

Ho Huichun. 1994. "Jin shinian lai Zhongguo jidujiaoshi yanjiu zongshu" (A review of studies on the history of Christianity in China by Chinese scholars in the last decade). In *Shijie Zongjiao Yanjiu* (Studies on World Religions) 4: 115–26.

Hobsbawn, E. J. 1994. "The Historian between the Quest for the Universal and the Quest for Identity." *Diogenes* 42, no. 4 (168): 51–63.

Hsing Fu-tsang. 1997. *Jidujiao xinyang yujiuguo shijian* (The Christian Faith and Its Application to China's National Salvation). Hong Kong: Alliance Seminary Press.

Irwin, D. T. 1991. "From One Story to Many: An Ecumenical Reappraisal of Church History." *Journal of Ecumenical Studies* 28 (fall): 537–54.

Jen Yu-wen. 1956. *Zhongguo Jidujiao di kaishan shiye* (Pioneers of the Protestant Church in China). Hong Kong: The Council on Christian Literature for Overseas Chinese.

Kalu, O. U. 1989. "African Church Historiography: An Ecumenical Perspective." *Encounter* 50, no. 1 (winter): 69–78.

———. 1998. " 'Jesus Christ, Where Are You?' Themes in West African Church Historiography." Unpublished.

Kappen, Sebastian. 1995. *Spirituality in the New Age of Recolonization.* Bangalore: Visthar.

Kenyatta, Jomo. [1938]. *Facing Mount Kenya.* With an Introduction by B. Malinowski. Reprinted New York: Vintage Books, n.d.

Kingsley, Mary. 1899. *West African Studies.* London: Macmillan.

Krapf, J. Ludwig. 1860. *Travels and Researches.* Boston: Tichnor and Fields.

Küng, Hans. 1964. "The Ecumenical Council by Human Convocation." In his *Structures of the Church.* New York: T. Nelson.

Kwok Pui-lan. 1992. *Chinese Women and Christianity, 1860–1927.* Atlanta: Scholars Press.

————. 1996. "Chinese Women and Protestant Christianity at the Turn of the Twentieth Century." In Daniel Bays, ed., *Christianity in China: From the Eighteenth Century to the Present.* Stanford: Stanford University Press, 194–208.

Latourette, Kenneth S. 1953. *A History of Christianity.* 2 vols. New York: Harper and Row; repr. 1975.

————. 1965. *A History of Christian Missions in China.* London: 1929. Reprint, Taipei: Cheng-wen Publishers.

Lee Kam-keung. 1997a. "Jidujiao gaigezhe — Huang Naishang yu Qingji gaige yundong" (The Christian Reformer: Huang Naishang and Late Qing Reform). *Sino-Humanitas* (Hong Kong Baptist University) 4: 189–212.

————. 1997b. "Xianggang huaren yu Zhongguo — He Qi, Hu Liyuan gean zhi tansuo" (Hong Kong Chinese and China: Case Studies of Ho Kai and Hu Liyuan). *Zhongguo shenxue yanjiuyuan qikan* (Hong Kong: The Chinese Graduate Seminary of Theology) 23: 53–71.

————. 1998. "Zhongguo jidujiaoshi yanjiu zhi xinqi jiqi fazhan" (The Rise and Development of Research on the History of Christianity in China). *Journal of the History of Christianity in Modern China.* Hong Kong: The Hong Kong Baptist University 1 (April): 5–30.

Lee Lai-to, ed. 1987. *The 1911 Revolution: The Chinese in British and Dutch Southeast Asia.* Singapore: Heinemann Asia.

Leung Yuen-sang. 1978. *Lin Lezhi cai hua shiye yu wanguo gongbao* (Young J. Allen in China: His careers and the Wanguo Gongbao). Hong Kong: Chinese University Press.

————. 1982. "Some Found It, Some Lost It: James Legge and the Three Chinese Boys from Malacca." *Asian Culture* (February 1983, Singapore) 1: 55–59.

————. 1987. "Religion and Revolution: The Response of the Singapore Chinese Christians toward the Revolutionary Movement in China." In Lee Lai-to, ed., *The Chinese in British and Dutch Southeast Asia.* Singapore: Heinemann Asia, 90–120.

Leung Yuen-sang, trans. 1994. *Dai Desheng: zhiai Zhonghua.* Sunnyville, Calif.: Christian Communications Ltd.

Lewis, Bernard, trans. and ed. 1987. *Islam: From the Prophet Muhammad to the Capture of Constantinople.* Vol. 2. New York: Oxford University Press.

Li Shiyue. 1962. *Fanyangjiao yundong* [The Anti-Christian Movement] (Beijing).

Lian Xi. 1997. *The Conversion of Missionaries: Liberalism in American Christian Missions in China.* University Park: Pennsylvania State University Press.

Lortz, Joseph. 1962 and 1965. *Geschichte der Kirche in Ideengeschichtlicher Betrachtung* [Church History from Idea-History Viewpoint]. 2 vols. Münster: Verlag Aschendorff.

Lu Shih-chiang. 1959–81. *Zhongguoguanshen fanjiao di yuanyin.* Taipei: Institute of Modern History, Academia Sinica.

Lutz, Jessie G. 1971. *China and the Christian Colleges, 1850–1950.* Ithaca, N.Y.: Cornell University Press.

————. 1988. *Chinese Politics and Christian Missions: The Anti-Christian Movement of 1920–28.* Notre Dame, Ind.: Cross Cultural Publications.

————. 1997. *Hakka Chinese Confront Protestant Christianity, 1850–1900.* Armonk, N.Y.: M. E. Sharpe.

————. 1998. "Chinese Christianity and Christian Missions: Western Literature — The State of the Field." *Journal of the History of Christianity in Modern China.* Hong Kong: The Hong Kong Baptist University, 1 (April): 31–54.

Lutz, Jessie G., and Rolland R. Lutz. 1995. "The Invisible China Missionaries: The Basel Mission's Chinese Evangelists, 1847–1866." *Mission Studies* 12 (October): 204–27.

Meersman, Achilles, O.F.M. 1963. Review of Trindade's book *Archivum Franciscanum Historicum* 56: 480.

Mundadan, A. M. 1984. *Indian Christians: Search for Identity and Struggle for Autonomy.* Bangalore: Dharmaram Publications.

————. 1997. *History and Beyond.* Aluva: Jeevass Publication.

————. 1998. *Paths of Indian Theology.* Bangalore: Dharmaram Publications.

Neill, Stephen. 1964a. *A History of Christian Missions,* Pelican History of the Church, vol. 6. Harmondsworth, U.K.: Penguin Books.

————. 1964b. *The Interpretation of the New Testament.* New York: Oxford University Press.

Ng, Peter. 1996. "Historical Archives in Chinese Christian Colleges before 1949." *International Bulletin of Missionary Research* 20, no. 3 (July): 106–8.

Njogu, Kimani. 1992. "Kenya: Grassroots Standardization of Swahili." In Nigel T. Crawhill, ed., *Democratically Speaking: International Perspectives on Language Planning.* Salt River, South Africa: National Language Project, November, 69–76.

Noll, M. A. 1996. "The Challenge of Contemporary Church History, the Dilemmas of Modern History, and Missiology to the Rescue." *Missiology: An International Review* 24, no. 1 (January): 47–64.

Norris, Richard. 1995. "The Fourteen Canons: Some Sidelong Critical Notes." In T. J. Wengert and C. B. Brockwell, eds., *Telling the Churches' Story: Ecumenical Perspectives on Writing Christian History.* Grand Rapids, Mich.: Eerdmans, 21–36.

Olson, Richard. 1993. *The Emergence of the Social Sciences, 1642–1792.* New York: Twayne Publishers.

Paik, George L. 1980. *The History of Protestant Missions in Korea, 1832–1910.* 3d ed. Seoul: Yonsei University Press.

Panikkar, Raimon. 1996. *The New Leader* 109, no. 6 (March): 25.

Paremmakkal, Thomas. 1971. *The Varthamanappusthakam, An Account of the History of the Malabar Church between the Years 1773 and 1786* [original in Malayalam, English translation with additional notes edited under the present title by P. J. Podipara, C.M.I.]. Rome: Institute of Oriental Studies.

Patrides, C. A. 1972. *The Grand Design of God. The Literary Form of the Christian View of History.* London: Routledge & Kegan Paul.

Paulinus of St. Bartholomew. 1794. *India Orientalis Christiana.* Rome: Typis Salo Monianis.

Peel, John. 1995. "For Who Hath Despised the Day of Small Things? Missionary Narratives and Historical Anthropology." *Journal for Comparative Study of Society and History* 37, no. 3 (July): 581–607.

Philip, T. V. 1972. "Conclusion." In H. C. Perumalil, C.M.I., and E. R. Hambye, S.J., eds. *Christianity in India: A History in Ecumenical Perspective.* Alleppey, S. India: Prakasam Publications, 300–301.

Pillay, G. J. 1988. "The Use of Functional-type Theories in the Study of Independent Christian Movements: A Critique." *Neue zeitschrift für missionswissenschaft* 44, no. 2: 125–35.

Porter, Andrew. 1997. "'Cultural Imperialism' and Protestant Missionary Enterprise, 1780–1914." *The Journal of Imperial and Commonwealth History* 25, no. 3 (September): 367–91.

Powicke, F. M. 1955. *Modern Historians and the Study of History.* London: Odhams Press Ltd.

Powles, C. H. 1984. "Christianity in the Third World: How Do We Study Its History? *Studies in Religion/Sciences Religieuses* 13 (2): 131–44.

Quinn, John R. 1997. "The Claims of the Primacy and the Costly Call to Unity." *Tanima* 5:59, 66.

Rahner, Karl. 1981. "Theological Interpretation of Vatican II." In *Theological Investigations.* Trans. Edward Quinn. London: Crossroad Publishing Company.

Robert, Dana L. 1994. "From Missions to Mission to Beyond Mission: The Historiography of American Protestant Foreign Missions Since World War II." *International Bulletin of Missionary Research* 1 (October): 146–62.

Robinson, J. H. 1920. *The New History: Essays Illustrating the Modern Historical Outlook.* New York: Macmillan.

Russell, H. O. 1985. "The Rewriting of Church History in the Third World." *Review and Expositor: A Baptist Theological Journal* 82 (Spring): 247–55.

Schlesinger, Arthur, Jr. 1974. "The Missionary Enterprise and Theories of Imperialism." In John K. Fairbank, ed., *The Missionary Enterprise in China and America.* Cambridge, Mass.: Harvard University Press, 336–73.

Scott, David C., ed. 1979. *Keshub Chunder Sen: A Selection.* Library of Indian Christian Theology, Companion Volume Series, No. 1. Bangalore: United Theological College.

Sharpe, J. 1991. "History from Below." In P. Burke, ed., *New Perspectives on Historical Writing.* Cambridge, U.K.: Polity Press, 24–41.

Sheldrake, P. 1992. *Spirituality and History. Questions of Interpretation and Method.* New York: Crossroad.

Shenk, Wilbert R. 1996. "Toward a Global Church History." *International Bulletin of Missionary Research* 20, no. 2 (April): 54.

Smith, Carl T. 1985. *Chinese Christians: Elites, Middlemen, and the Church in Hong Kong.* Hong Kong: Oxford University Press.

de Souza, Francisco, S.J. 1710. *Oriente Conquistado a Jesú Christo...* (Lisbon). New edition by M. Lopes de Almeida. Porto: Pello e Irmão — Editores, 1978.

Stanley, Brian. 1992. *The History of the Baptist Missionary Society, 1792–1992.* Edinburgh: T. & T. Clark.

Tang Xiaobing. 1996. *Global Space and the Nationalist Discourse of Modernity: The Historical Thinking of Liang Qichao*. Stanford: Stanford University Press, 231.

Tao Feiya. 1998. "1949 nian yilai guonei Zhongguo jidujiaoshi yanjiu shuping" (A state-of-the-field paper on the history of Chinese Christianity in the PRC since 1949). *Journal of the History of Christianity in Modern China* 1:56–67.

Taylor, Dr. and Mrs. Howard. 1919. *Hudson Taylor and China Inland Mission*. London: China Inland Mission.

Templeman, G. 1976. *The Neglect of the Past and the Price It Exacts*. London: University of London.

de Trindade, Paulo. 1962–1967. 3 vols. Felix Lopes, ed., *Conquista Espiritual do Oriente; em que se dá relaçao de algumas cousas mais notáveis que fizeram os Frades Menoren da Santa Provincia de S. Tomé da India Oriental em a pregaçào da fé e conversao dos infiéis, em main de trinta reinos, do Cabo de Boa Esperança até as remotissimaa Ilhas do Japào*. Lisbon: OFM.

Tucker, Ruth. 1992. "Colorizing Church History." *Christianity Today* 36, no. 8 (July): 20–23.

Veyssière de La Croze, Mathurin. 1724. *Histoire du Christianisme aux Indes*. Le Hay: Aux Defens de la Compagnie.

Walker, Williston. 1985. *A History of the Christian Church*. 4th ed. Revised by Richard A. Norris, David W. Lotz, Robert T. Handy. New York: Scribners. First published 1918.

Walls, Andrew F. 1987. "The Christian Tradition in Today's World." In Frank Whaling, ed., *Religion in Today's World*. Edinburgh: T. & T. Clark, 76–109.

———. 1991. "Structural Problems in Mission Studies." *International Bulletin of Missionary Research* 15, no. 4 (October): 146–55. Reprinted in *The Missionary Movement in Christian History*. Maryknoll, N.Y.: Orbis Books, 1996, 143–59.

———. 1996. *The Missionary Movement in Christian History*. Maryknoll, N.Y.: Orbis Books.

Wang Lixin. 1997. *Meiguo Chuanjiaoshi yu wanqing Zhongguo xiandaihua* (American Missionaries and Modernization in Late Qing China). Tianjin: Renmin Chubanshe.

Warren, Max. 1965. *The Missionary Movement from Britain in Modern History*. London: SCM Press.

Webster, John C. B. 1978. "The History of Christianity in India: Aims and Method." *Bangalore Theological Forum* 10. 110–48.

Wengert, T. J., and C. B. Brockwell, Jr., eds. 1995. *Telling the Churches' Story: Ecumenical Perspectives on Writing Christian History*. Grand Rapids, Mich.: Eerdmans.

Wesseling, Hank. 1991. "Overseas History." In Peter Burke, ed., *New Perspectives on Historical Writings*. Cambridge, U.K.: Polity Press, 67–92.

Westermann, Diedrich. 1925. "Place and Function of the Vernacular in African Education." *International Review of Missions* (January): 25–36.

Williams, C. H. 1938. *The Modern Historian*. London: Thomas Nelson & Sons.

Wong Man Kong, and Lee Ka Kui. 1994. *Dangdai Xianggang shixue yanjiu* (Contemporary historical studies in Hong Kong), ed. Society of Modern Chinese History in Hong Kong. Hong Kong: San-lian Shu-tian, 148–68.

Woodward, C. Vann. 1989. *The Future of the Past*. New York: Oxford University Press.

Xi Lian. 1997. *The Conversion of Missionaries: Liberalism in American Protestant Missions in China, 1907–1932*. University Park: Pennsylvania State University Press.

Yeh Jen-chang. 1992. *Wusi yihou di fandui Jidujiao yundong* (The Anti-Christian Movement after the May Fourth Movement). Taipei: Jiuda wenhua gufen gongxi.

Yip Ka-che. 1980. *Religion, Nationalism, and Chinese Students: The Anti-Christian Movement of 1922–1927*. Bellingham: Western Washington University Press.

Select Bibliography
on Global Historiography

Ajayi, J. F. Ade, and E. A. Ayandele. 1969. "Writing African Church History." In Peter Beyerhaus and Carl F. Hallencreutz, eds., *The Church Crossing Frontiers: Essays on the Nature of Mission*. Uppsala: Gleerup, 90–108.

Amirtham, Samuel, and Cyris H. S. Moon, eds. 1987. *The Teaching of Ecumenics*. Geneva: WCC Publications.

CEHILA. n.d. *Materiales para una Historia de la Teología en América Latina*. San José, Costa Rica: CEHILA.

————. 1975. *Para una historia de la Iglesia en América Latina*. Barcelona: Editorial Nova Terra.

————. 1977. *Para una historia de la evangelización en América Latina*. Barcelona: Editorial Nova Terra.

Church History Association of India (CHAI). 1974. "A Scheme for a Comprehensive History of Christianity in India." *Indian Church History Review* 8:89–90.

Clifford, James. 1980. "The Translation of Cultures." *Journal of Pacific History* 15, no. 1: 2–20.

Cohen, Paul A. 1984. *Discovering History in China: American Historical Writings on the Recent Chinese Past*. New York: Columbia University Press.

Daniels, David D. 1993. "Teaching the History of U.S. Christianity in a Global Perspective." *Theological Education* 29, no. 2 (spring): 91–111.

Dussel, Enrique. 1988. "Future of Missions in the Third Millennium." *Mission Studies* 5, no. 2 (10): 66–89.

————, ed. 1992. *The Church in Latin America, 1492–1992*. Maryknoll, N.Y.: Orbis Books.

Fairbank, John K. 1969. "Assignment for the '70s." *American Historical Review* 74, no. 3 (February): 861–79.

Gonzalez, Justo L. 1993. "Globalization in the Teaching of Church History." *Theological Education* 29, no. 2 (spring): 49–71.

Hallencreutz, Carl F. 1993. "Third World Church History — An Integral Part of Theological Education." *Studia Theologica* 47: 29–47.

Hutchinson, Mark, and Ogbu Kalu, eds. 1998. *A Global Faith: Essays on Evangelicalism and Globalization*. Sydney: Centre for the Study of Australian Christianity.

Irvin, Dale T. 1998. *Christian Histories, Christian Traditioning: Rendering Accounts*. Maryknoll, N.Y.: Orbis Books.

————, and Scott W. Sunquist. 2001. *History of the World Christian Movement*. Vol. 1: *Earliest Christianity to 1453*. Maryknoll, N.Y.: Orbis Books.

Jedin, Hubert. 1965. "General Introduction to Church History." In *Handbook of Church History*. New York: Herder and Herder, 1–56.

Jenkins, Philip. *The Next Christendom: The Coming of Global Christianity*. New York: Oxford University Press, 2002.

Kalu, Ogbu K., ed. 1985. *African Church Historiography: An Ecumenical Perspective*. Papers presented at a Workshop on African Church History held in Nairobi, August 3–8. Bern: Evangelische Arbeitsstelle Oekumene Schweiz.

Klaiber, Jeffrey. 1990. "Toward a New History of the Church in the Third World." *International Bulletin of Missionary Research* 14, no. 3 (July): 105–8.

Korschorke, Klaus, ed. 1998. *"Christen und Gewurze": Konfrontation und Interaktion Kolonialer und indigener Christentumsvarianten*. Göttingen: Vandenhoeck und Ruprecht. Essays in German and English.

Leff, Gordon. 1969. *History and Social Theory*. Tuscaloosa: University of Alabama.

Mundadan, A. Mathias. 1986. "Six Volume Project of Church History Association of India." *East Asia Journal of Theology* 4: 175–77.

Philip, T. V. 1987. "Church History in Ecumenical Perspective." In Samuel Amirtham and Cyris H. S. Moon, eds., *The Teaching of Ecumenics*. Geneva: WCC Publications, 42–53.

Ranger, T. O., ed. 1968. *Emerging Themes of African History*. Proceedings of the International Congress of African Historians. Nairobi: East African Publishing House.

————, and I. N. Kimambo, eds. 1972. *The Historical Study of African Religion*. Berkeley and Los Angeles: University of California Press.

Robert, Dana L. 2000. "Shifting Southward: Global Christianity since 1945." *International Bulletin of Missionary Research* 24, no. 2 (April): 50–58.

Roxborogh, John. 1991. "Whose History and Whose Theology? Reflections from Malaysia on the Study of Christianity in the Non-western World." *Mission Studies* 8, no. 1 (15): 93–103.

Sanneh, Lamin. 1989. *Translating the Message: The Missionary Impact on Culture*. Maryknoll, N.Y.: Orbis Books.

————. 1990. "Mission and the Modern Imperative — Retrospect and Prospect: Charting a Course." In Joel A. Carpenter and Wilbert R. Shenk, eds., *Earthen Vessels: American Evangelicals and Foreign Missions, 1880–1980*. Grand Rapids, Mich.: Eerdmans, 301–16.

————. 1995. "World Christianity and the Study of History." *Reflections* (winter-spring): 1–10.

Schumacher, John. 1971. "The 'Third World' and the Self-Understanding of the Twentieth-Century Church." *Concilium: The Self-Understanding of the Church* 7, no. 7 (September): 102–11.

Shenk, Wilbert R. 1996. "Toward a Global Church History." *International Bulletin of Missionary Research* 20, no. 2 (April): 50–57.

Spindler, M. R. 1990. "Writing African Church History (1969–1989): A Survey of Recent Studies." *Exchange* 19, no. 1 (April): 70–87.

Strayer, Robert. 1976. "Mission History in Africa: New Perspectives on an Encounter." *African Studies Review* 19, no. 1 (April): 1–15.

Thunberg, Lars. 1969. "Redemption for the Wrongs of History." In Peter Beyerhaus and Carl F. Hallencreutz, eds., *The Church Crossing Frontiers: Essays on the Nature of Mission*. Uppsala: Gleerup, 209–25.

Verstraelen, Frans J. 1997. "Southern Perspectives on Christian History." *Neue Zeitschrift für Missionswissenschaft* 53, no. 2: 99–113.

Vischer, Lukas, ed. 1982. *Church History in an Ecumenical Perspective*. Papers and Reports of an International Ecumenical Consultation held in Basle, October 12–17, 1981. Bern: Evangelische Arbeitsstelle Oekumene Schweiz.

———. 1985. *Towards a History of the Church in the Third World: The Issue of Periodization*. Papers and Reports of a Consultation (July 1983, Geneva). Bern: Evangelische Arbeitsstelle Oekumene Schweiz.

Von Laue, Theodore H. 1987. *The World Revolution of Westernization: The Twentieth Century in Global Perspective*. New York: Oxford University Press.

Walls, A. F. 1976. "Towards Understanding Africa's Place in Christian History." In J. S. Pobee, ed., *Religion in a Pluralistic Society*. Leiden: E. J. Brill, 180–89.

Webster, John C. B. 1978. "The History of Christianity in India: Aims and Methods." *Bangalore Theological Forum* 10, no. 2: 110–48.

Wengert, Timothy J., and Charles W. Brockwell, Jr., eds. 1995. *Telling the Churches' Stories: Ecumenical Perspectives on Writing Christian History*. Grand Rapids, Mich.: Eerdmans.

Index